Colonel Worthington's Shiloh

Colonel Worthinton's Shiloh

The Tennessee Campaign, 1862
by an officer of the
Ohio Volunteers

T. Worthington

LEONAUR

Colonel Worthington's Shiloh
The Tennessee Campaign, 1862
by an officer of the Ohio Volunteers
by T. Worthington

First published 1872 under the title
Shiloh: or the Tennessee Campaign of 1862

Leonaur is an imprint of Oakpast Ltd

ISBN: 978-1-84677-674-8 (hardcover)
ISBN: 978-1-84677-673-1 (softcover)

http://www.leonaur.com

Contents

BADEAU'S MAP OF SHILOH.

Corrected by GRANT and SHERMAN, being the dotted lines. - - - - - - - - - - - -

Corrected by W. P. G.—(See Nos. 1–5, 10 and 12.)

Scale of two miles.   Figures 10 to 29.

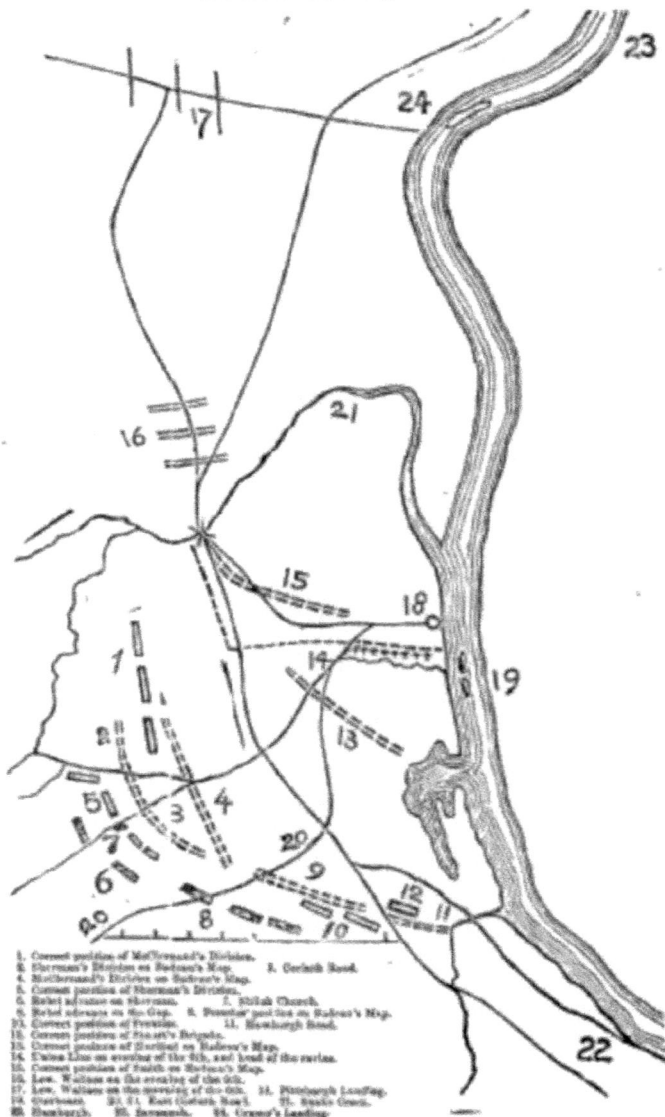

1. Correct position of McClernand's Division.
2. Sherman's Division on Badeau's Map.   3. Corinth Road.
4. McClernand's Division on Badeau's Map.
5. Correct position of Sherman's Division.
6. Rebel advance on Sherman.   7. Shiloh Church.
8. Rebel advance on the Gap.   9. Prentiss' position on Badeau's Map.
10. Correct position of Prentiss.   11. Hamburgh Road.
12. Correct position of Stuart's Brigade.
13. Union Line on evening of the 6th, and head of the ravine.
14. Correct position of Hurlbut on Badeau's Map.
15. Correct position of Smith on Badeau's Map.
16. Lew. Wallace on the evening of the 6th.
17. Lew. Wallace on the morning of the 6th.   18. Pittsburgh Landing.
19. Overborn.   20, 21. East Corinth Road.   21. Snake Creek.
22. Hamburgh.   23. Savannah.   24. Crump's Landing.

Written especially for the Army of the Tennessee in 1862 and for the friends and relatives of those patriot soldiers, who sank into their graves on Shiloh's field

Unknelled, unnoticed, and unknown.

I believe every life lost that day was necessary. Sherman.

Bury the dead on the field wherever they fell. Same.

by a comrade on that battlefield and a West Point Graduate of 1827.

To the thousands of union soldiers, who alone held their ground at Shiloh, and hold it yet, the victims of negligence, or the martyrs of design, admiration and gratitude for the sacrifice they offered up, and with regret for all who fell in what they believed to be a righteous cause. This imperfect commentary is dedicated by by a comrade in battle and a West Point Graduate of 1827.

Washington, D.C., April, 1872.

Advertisement

The writer of the following compendium, fully intending to have it published about the 1st of April, 1862, was not assured till the last week in March of overt acts, by direction of a cabal in Washington, to protract the operations of an invading army, though at the imminent risk, and indeed certainty, of defeat and slaughter of myriads of the Union troops. This occasioned his having to reject over half he had written, and rewrite nearly the whole work.

In the first week of April, after long search, he got together Halleck's dispatches of March 3rd and 4th, plainly pointing to the instruments chosen for this purpose of interested desolation. This required further changes in the chapters, and may account for many points obscure and inconsistent, which may be corrected hereafter, if this commentary is found worthy of notice.

He has been refused all information at the War Department, as the policy of protracting the war required the suppression or destruction of all special army records, and the abrogation of all established principles of military law.

W. P. G.

Washington, April, 1872.

Explanation of Halleck's Dispatches of March 3rd and 4th

The writer, on consideration and advice, that not one intelligent reader in a thousand would take any notice of the peculiarly opposite statements in Halleck's dispatches of March 4, 1862, has thought best to make an explanation. The whole of the dispatch of March 4, from Halleck to Buell, is given to show the extent of the fraud.

General Buell to General Halleck.

Nashville, March 3, 1862.

General Halleck, St. Louis:

What can I do to aid your operations against Columbus? Remember, I am separated from you by the Tennessee river. Johnson is moving toward Decatur and burning the bridges as he goes.

D. C. Buell.

General Halleck to General Buell.

St. Louis, March 4, 1862.

General Buell, Nashville:

If Johnson has destroyed the railroad and bridges in his rear, he cannot return to attack you. Why not come to the Tennessee and operate with me to cut Johnson's line with Memphis, Randolph, and New Madrid. Columbus has been evacuated and destroyed. Enemy is concentrating at New Madrid and Island No 10. I am concentrating a force of twenty thousand against him. Grant with all available force has gone up the Tennessee, to destroy connection at Corinth, Jackson, and Humboldt. Estimated strength of enemy at New Madrid, Randolph, and Memphis is fifty thousand. It is of vital importance to separate them from Johnson's army. Come over to Savannah or Florence, and we can do it. We then can operate on Decatur or Memphis, or both, as may appear best.

H. W. Halleck.

This is an entirely deceptive, and in part fictitious dispatch, with false information of a trebly criminal character.

1st. No expedition had gone up the Tennessee, nor did for a week after the 4th.

2nd. There was no intention of cutting railroad communication at Corinth, Jackson, and Humboldt, or any of those places, which were to be let alone especially.

3rd. It was not the intention (though he says of vital importance) to cut communication between A. S. Johnson and Memphis, but to leave the way open for an object, and a base one.

4th. It was not Halleck's intention that Buell should march to Florence, when urging him to "come over" to that place, but to stop the march, as he did.

5th. It is seen he does not notify Buell that he has displaced Grant as commander of the Tennessee expedition; but, on the contrary, having displaced him, (as a sham or cover,) tells Buell he has gone up the Tennessee with an expedition that did not start for a week after the date of the dispatch, and then under the command of C. F. Smith, as a cover.

For any one of these acts of falsehood or deception, and especially for the false information, Halleck's life should have been forfeited; and were he alive now any President fit for his position would, on the discovery of such conduct, drop him from the rolls of the army in disgrace. Yet this man, because capable of such gross criminality, was virtually the director of the war from November, 1861, till it was over. Whatever were the particulars of the bargain between Halleck and the Washington cabal, it was a diabolical transfer of each to the other on both sides, Halleck having and keeping the advantage. Those dispatches should be in the War Office, but the War Office dare not make them known officially without betrayal of the whole plot. And thus the War Office is stopped from giving any information whatever as to any event of the war, while the present Administration (1872) is in power; and when it is out, all records of that campaign will have disappeared—most have now. No such criminal occurrence is upon historical record, and no monarch on earth dare trifle with the lives and treasure of the people as this plot proves the people of this Union have been trifled with, cheated, and deceived by the war administration in 1862, and no doubt during the war.

The main object was to deceive Buell, and to effect, not prevent, the junction of Johnson with Beauregard at Corinth. Buell had for three months been urging the seizure of Florence, and by consequence the occupation of the upper Tennessee, which would have captured Chattanooga and Knoxville with scarce an effort. He was, therefore, anxious to see some use made of the Tennessee river for the furtherance of the war. He had in his command over 100,000 men, doing next to nothing. Grant, Halleck, and Sherman had been together some days, according to Badeau, the last week in January, 1862, at St. Louis, when the outlines of the intrigue, of which the dispatches following furnish ample evidence, were then and there doubtless agreed upon, under instructions or contracts from Washington, inclosed of course to Halleck, who was really "commander-in-chief" from and after the time he left Washington for St. Louis, in November, 1861, and came on as such in July, 1862.

The seeming quarrel initiated between the chiefs of the jobbers would operate to silence future suspicion. Hence the dispatch to the War Office of the 3rd, and the dispatch of the 4th to Grant, at Fort Henry, both intended for deceptive purposes, of which there is ample evidence, but for which there is here no room, even if, to a professional soldier, the deception was not plain upon the face of these productions of "Old Brains"

(Halleck.) These dispatches, to be found in *Grant's Badeau*, page 59, excited exceeding surprise and sympathy for Grant among innocent historians, such as Mansfield, &c. Grant was but nominally out of command, to cover up the intrigue, one of its results being Shiloh and its slaughter.

Smith, as has been stated, was put in command to cover the plan of getting Sidney Johnson past Florence, as fast as possible, to Corinth. This, of course, would have been prevented if the expedition that stopped at Savannah on the 11th had kept on up that day to Florence, the point where the Charleston and Memphis railroad reaches the Tennessee river, near the foot of the Muscle Shoals, the head of river navigation, connected by railroad with Decatur, Alabama, where Johnson then was, March 11, 1862, about to move west. This stoppage at Savannah brought on the battle of Shiloh. The subsequent events of the campaign, and those of the war, plainly show the collusion between these officers themselves in the field, and some authority at Washington having the regulation of the campaign.

How, then, is it possible or appropriate for a historian, and much less for a mere compiler, to maintain the proper "dignity of history" when dealing with such mountebanks and their intrigues? And to have invested such men in such a way, and by such means, with almost absolute power over the lives and limbs of hundreds of thousands of patriotic and unsuspecting citizens, is one of the most criminal and terrible episodes in the warlike annals of the world.

A marble monument cannot be constructed of mud, or even unburnt brick. These three men had already shown how really worthless, for military enterprises, they were; yet these three men have held the most prominent positions in the war of the rebellion, not by really legitimate authority, however it seemed such, but plainly, as events have proved, by a collusion, which implies criminality by some authority at Washington never perhaps to be perfectly developed; but it should be answered for. Caligula invested his horse with the consulship; Domitian triumphed for his defeat by the Dacians, as Sherman has been heroised for misconduct at Shiloh; and Shakspeare makes Mark Antony treat his colleague, the simple soldier Lepidus, as nothing more than a well-trained war-horse. But this did not make the horse of the tyrant an able general, nor Domitian a great commander: no more did Shiloh make more than a sham of Sherman, nor did the words of Antony abate the merits of Lepidus as an able soldier. The elevation of these three men, as the fitting instruments for party objects, made them nothing more than leaders for the time to carry out dishonest purposes. And they can only hold their ill-gotten reputations, now waning fast away, so long as the deception is maintained, by a prevention of all investigation. Into this general investigation they dare not go, nor into the slightest specifications against them in this imperfect commentary.

If they do not now express a willingness to go into such investigation, everything herein stated or charged must be proven by default, as almost everything so charged is proven by their own reports and letters, and the histories, of which they themselves have declared themselves to he the true authority. The repression or destruction of all the usual war records in relation to Shiloh was the result of that protractive policy of which these men were the instruments. They have been suppressed or destroyed; if not, let these records be produced. Much of the true history of the campaign was suppressed by the suspension of the 34th article of the army regulations by Sherman, and perhaps other commanders in the field.[1]

Let these facts, then, be borne in mind by the professional reader, who may condemn, as in bad taste, any badinage or jocularity, at the expense of these men, (mere upholstery made-up commanders,) and consider that the Government, during the war, has turned over for the consideration of the historian little else than mere pretenders and mountebanks, carried through the war at the expense and indulgence of the nation, in spite of

---

1. The record of Buell's court of inquiry was not allowed to extend back of nor to include Shiloh, and that is gone; and a court record touching the trial of Colonel Worthington, 46th Ohio, has been entirely suppressed; and no order-books at the War Office are allowed examination by any one.

themselves and blunders: their admirers and parasites not even believing in their own letters and reports, however derogatory to their characters as honest men and good soldiers, as this treatise will demonstrate. The writer, who claims nothing of the dignity of a historian, may mingle comical remarks to relieve his too tragical compilations, in which last he has indulged as little as truth will permit. No historian, at any rate, is bound down to the "dignity of history," where the subjects offered afford no dignity in words or acts or character, on which to expatiate. He then considers that he may, therefore, be permitted the occasional expression of contempt and indignation, of which, for their acts and omissions, every honest mind must be conscious, and a professional soldier would be a hypocrite, such expression to suppress.

W. P. G.

Which may pass, when seen, for West Point Graduate.

Prefatorial

A synopsis of the Shiloh campaign. How Halleck exposes his own intrigue.

General Halleck to the War Office at Washington.

St. Louis, March 3, 1862.

General Grant left his command without my authority and went to Nashville. I can get no returns or reports of any kind from him. I am tired and worn-out by this neglect and inefficiency. (*The very qualities wanted by the junto. 1st, act of the jugglers, &c. W. P. G.*)

Halleck to Grant.

St. Louis, March 4, 1862.[1]

General U. S. Grant:

You will place General Smith in command of the Tennessee expedition and remain yourself at Fort Henry. Why do you not obey my orders to report strength and position of your command? H. W. Halleck. (*2nd act of the jugglers*)

General Halleck to General Buell.

St. Louis, March 4, 1862[2]

Grant, with all available force, has gone up the Tennessee, to destroy (railroad) connection at Corinth, Jackson, and Humboldt." (*All humbug, as the above dispatches prove. W. P. G. 3rd act of the jugglers, by Halleck, Grant, and Sherman.*)

2. Observe the dates.
3. Idem

17

The originators and managers of this performance were in Washington, and may yet appear on this bloody stage, as it afterwards got to be.

No expedition went up from Fort Henry till the 10th March, in temporary command of Smith, for a special purpose of the juggler. On the 11th Grant is in command again, and writes to Smith, March 11, 1862, (from Fort Henry:)

General Halleck telegraphs that when reinforcements arrive I may take the general direction. I think it doubtful if I shall accept. (*Certainly not; but he did accept, as usual, having only been out of the comedy behind the scenes. The jugglers will next appear between Shiloh, Pittsburgh, and Savannah. W. P. G., West Point Graduate.*)

A very distinguished Senator, who runs the financial machinery of the nation with more or less ability and stability, has very justly remarked, in terms, that there was no very specific difference or distinction between a tariff or revenue and one for protection, they being convertible terms.

The same may be said, in some sort, of the relation between a preface and an introduction, as they invariably run into each other. This writer, being nothing more than a compiler of facts and fictions, thrown carelessly together, must leave the reader, if he have one, to arrange what may be written where he chooses, calling it either preface or introduction. The following treatise, compilation, or commentary, is written, in the first place, because the writer could find no one else who would undertake it, who would attempt it, or who was willing to undertake, or have any share or responsibility in such a production. This writing, then, was Hobson's choice on the part of the writer, and it must be on the part of the reader, until some regular arid competent historian can take up the chaos herein thrown together, and arrange the same in proper historical shape.

The work was compiled under very peculiar circumstances. It was necessary that some part of the expense should be met by prepaid subscriptions, as some of the ablest newspapers are carried on. Canvassing for subscriptions and prepayments, it was at once apparent that, in everybody's opinion, a true history of "Shiloh" would, of necessity, be taken and considered as an attack upon those officers who had, and have, and claim, the honour, and the merit, and the gratitude of the people for that "brilliant success" of April 6, 1862. This "brilliant success" had been most remarkable for the almost miraculous manner in which the Union army and its commanders had been snatched from the wide-opened jaws of destruction, late in the afternoon of April 6, as so forcibly related by General Grant himself in his report of April 10, 1862.

In the necessary connection between this providential deliverance, after the peculiar occurrences of the day, and the peculiar conduct of the Union commanders, consisted the elements of the inevitably supposed attack on these officers. However this may be, the writer is bound to impute to the prospect of such an attack the facility with which sufficient ammunition was subscribed to make it. His deepest acknowledgements are, therefore, due to Generals Grant and Sherman. For it is very certain that but for an anxious, or curious, or interested, or disinterested disposition to see the result of such an attack, real or supposed, the means of commencing it would not have been had. This humble compiler utterly disclaims any intention of such an attack, for the sake of the attack; has no more idea of an attack on these officers than they had of an attack on Johnson and Beauregard at Shiloh, though Buell's troops were at hand, which would have made the attack, at Hamburgh or Shiloh, a "brilliant success" with scarce the scratch of a butcher's bill on either side.

To quote from *Sherman's Campaigns* by Bowman, "this history of the Shiloh campaign is written in the single interest of truth;" and Cicero, it is said, somewhere inculcates, that in writing history we must not fear to relate what is true, nor dare to state for truth anything which is the reverse. So far as regards the Shiloh campaign, this law of history has been so far, reversed by all writers on the subject.

To follow this rule, where the sources of truth have been poisoned or perverted, is for the time, and often forever, impossible, as will prove the history of the late war. Take, for instance, General Grant's report of Shiloh, which says as little as possible, and that little is in general fallacious, and so intended to be. It is not so much an expression, as a suppression of facts and incidents.

1st. "On Sunday morning our pickets were attacked and driven in by the enemy."

Here, then, is as suppression of the facts, that our pickets had been driven within half a mile of the camp at 7 a. m., on the day before the battle, and at least one of our picket posts within easy cannon shot of the camp had been occupied by the enemy. That for several days there had been in his immediate front not less than 60,000 hostile troops, according to his estimate and belief. That he had, nevertheless, early on the morning of the 5th of April, withdrawn his cavalry pickets and artillery from the front or Sherman's line, and had no detachments of any kind out that day to the distance of over two and a half miles, where the enemy had been found on the 4th in such force as to make General Sherman apprehensive of an immediate attack. That, in fact, he and that commander had had reason to expect an attack from and after the afternoon of the 3rd of April, 1862.

2nd. To make known and not to conceal facts, he should have stated that General Buell, of the Army of the Ohio, from Nashville, had arrived at 5 p. m. of the 5th, and the 1st division of his army about noon the same day. That, as had been intended, these troops might have been thrown up to Hamburgh, on the river, four miles above, where they would have been little over a mile to the right and rear of the rebel army. That this was not done, for the reason that General Halleck was daily expected, and it had been his anxious desire to gratify that innocent commander's disposition to lead personally in the expected attack. That, knowing of General Buell's vicinity, it was preposterous to suppose there would have been any real attack by the enemy, in which he was supported by the experienced and able conviction of General Sherman, as expressed to Major Kicker, which conviction was, that "Beauregard was not such a fool as to march all the way from Corinth to make such an attack," and still persisted in the conviction that Beauregard made a fatal mistake when he made an attack which drove us back no farther than the landing, with the loss of but 10,000 men, or only half the number of those that "did not run away" inclusive, &c., in the first day's fight. Had he stated this, and several other items to be supplied by this commentary, his report might have been of at least as much value to general history as Sherman's letter of January, 1865, to the U. S. S. Magazine is to Sherman and Grant's history, if at all credible.

To do the commander of the Army of the Tennessee entire credit, it must be admitted that we may gather by deep enough research that General Buell's arrival (5 p. m.) saved the landing and transports from capture and the array from an equivalent conclusion of the campaign, but most readers might, with justice, suppose that General Buell was a delinquent subordinate like General Wallace, who had tardily got up from his usual position on the field, as G. charged and charges on Buell to this day. Now, these suppressions dam up, to say the least, the true source of history, while his statement of facts does as much to pervert the same fountains to wrong conclusions. He knew the gunboats were useless without the presence of Buell's troops, and were and could only be effective by the excitement of a cannonade.

The statement that his force was too much fatigued to perfect a victory which was lost by neglect of pursuit, is alike "fallacious, as there were over 30,000 men, not in action that day, ready, and anxious, and able to pursue all night. If he had sent 3,000 idle cavalry and 10,000 of the stragglers and idlers even, without ammunition, as most of them were, up to Hamburgh at any time after the arrival of Buell, all the trains and most of the rebel troops would have been captured. But this was not then the object. They were saved for future use, as the wise old hunter spares the she wolf as productive of wolf scalps when at a premium. The enemy, he says, retreated in good order, for which he had, or should have had, an expression of their obligations, properly engrossed, in the neatest style, &c.

The worst perversion, however, is the statement 1st. That General Sherman was with his command the entire two days of the battle, (which Sherman's report denies.) 2nd. That he displayed great judgement and skill in the management of his troops, (which the report further denies.) 3rd. The repetition that his place was never vacant. 4th. That he was twice wounded and had three horses killed under him, (*all by agreement. W. P. G.*)

These statements are all disposed of by General Sherman's report and his (Grant's) autobiography by Badeau.

And thus:

1. General Sherman states in his report that at 10 a.m. his 3rd brigade (Hildebrand's) had substantially disappeared from the field, and that the other two, Buckland's and McDowell's, 4th and 1st, were conducted by his aids "to join on McClernand's right." This point was over a mile off at the time. It gradually grew to near three miles, but the brigades never joined McClernand's right, and Sherman never joined the brigades: so that, if that part of Sherman's report be true, and Buckland's report be true that his brigade was dispersed at 9 a.m., and Sherman's report be true that the attack in force did not commence till 8 a. m. of the 6th, Sherman was with his command, by his own report, but one hour of the two days; and there were and are thousands of witnesses, besides Sherman's report? to prove this, Buckland's report aside.

2. If Sherman displayed such great skill and judgement whence arise so many statements, by most historians who heroise him, that his troops were all dispersed by 8 or 9 a.m.; and what was that skill and judgement worth in his own opinion, which deferred to that of subordinate officers, (his aids,) to whom he consigned, he says, his only two organized brigades at 10 a. m.

By this he plainly intimated, 1st. That these troops were safer in the hands of his aids than under his own command; or, 2nd. That he was safer in avoiding the command of these troops on a march during which a contest he knew was inevitable, as the result proved.

Take either horn, and what is proven as to "this gallant and able officer" more meritorious than that he exhibited the modesty of Bob or Tom Acres in the one case, in want of self-confidence, or the wisdom of the great Falstaff in the other in the husbandry of discretion.

The truth of this statement, as to the present commander-in-chief, is easier sustained in this case than usual, as the writer can bear witness that McDowell's brigade was thus detached out of Sherman's immediate command by himself, in the hottest of the fight, and it was most fortunate in his discretion of giving up the command, as stated by him, and perhaps equally so in its desertion by his aids and his friend and favourite, the brigade commander, which left it, as admiring historians say, "far to the right, and front of the Union army," to join, as ordered, on to McClernand's perpetually vanishing right, if allowed by the enemy, who vetoed the procedure before it came in sight of the objective vanished point; and about the time that Sherman, like Horatius Codes (or perhaps Cokely) at the Sublician bridge, was so highly commended by Grant, (so S. says,) for so obstinately keeping back the enemy without troops, except his sword, as Mrs. P's broom kept out the ocean, or the North sea, all the same.

3. The repetition that his place, or the position of his feet, or his horse's feet, was never vacant, is perhaps true, under the construction of the way in which a leopard may change his spots; of which construction, if his report is credible, he took advantage, by his change, in retreat, of the numerous spots between Shiloh church in the morning and Snake creek bridge at night.

4. As the latest reports are' considered most reliable, Grant's statement, on Badeau's authority, may be found on page 84 of that veracious chronicle, that at the close of the battle Grant was struck, but not hurt; Sherman was slightly wounded, very slightly, in the epidermis, left hand, on its back, by a twig, and at least 10,000 men on each side were either killed or wounded, (true;) in which there is some slight show of truth as to the mortal hurts of these greatest of rebellion-risen commanders, while not

much is abated of the slaughter they achieved. And to sum up all the true material for history above stated, as derived from Grant and Sherman's reports, we have, 1st. That Buell's army saved the Army of the Tennessee from ruin on the 6th April; 2nd. Sherman gave up all command at 9 or 10 a. m. of the first day's fight, and was slightly wounded, he says. As to the three horses, their bones, if ever discovered, will be just as recognizable as those of the thousands of Union soldiers dumped down and but slightly covered, under or over where they fell, "unknelled, unnoticed, and unknown," by the benevolence of this "prototype of Washington," who has the promulgation of the veracious Sherman for being as " unselfish, kind hearted, and honest as a man should be." And now, having presented for true history all found worthy of transcription as truth from Grant's report, return we, as the French say, to our *mouton*, or to General Sherman's historian, Colonel S. M. Bowman, say "longbow-man" for shortness.

This historian, in the "single interest of truth," concludes his preface by the hope, that his efforts in so deep an interest may elicit new testimony from the same depths. Now, if it be in the interest of truth to detect fallacy and expose fiction, something of the sort, it is hoped, will be perfected by the digressions and commentaries required in the search of that oldest inhabitant of the bottom of a well. And, to begin at the beginning, let all historians of the Shiloh campaign, past and future, be warned against the report of Grant, repeatedly contradicted by himself, and as is seen, by Sherman's report at the time. Be warned against Sherman's report, contradictory in itself, and afterwards contradicted by himself; and especial care must be taken to exclude as truth everything Halleck has so far advanced, or which yet, undiscovered, may be advanced on his authority, granting that the evidence of these men may be used against themselves.

No living man, as he perhaps may repeat, regrets General Halleck's death more deeply than this narrator. He might, if alive, be made to answer for some part of the mischief he has done, by being compelled to make known his authority for the many terrible and most diabolical incidents of the war, before and after he became commander-in-chief of the army at Washington. Whitelaw Reid's paper is the most readable account of the battle, and he seems to have had an inkling of design in the arrangements for defeat he has remarked were seemingly made. He was doubtless deceived by some one in Sherman's interest as to the position, of McClernand's left brigade, as to the attack upon the 1st brigade before the first retreat, and its disappearance among the ravines of Snake creek, &c., &c.

He might have seen that it was detached in that direction by Sherman's report, but he never had any means of further tracing its operations. As to his statement that Grant allowed no sign of distrust to escape him, he had not seen Grant's letter to Buell about noon of the 6th, of which the following extract is sufficient at present:

> Commanding Officer, &c., Buell's army, near Pittsburgh:
> If you will get upon the field, leaving all your baggage over the river, it will be a move to our advantage, and possibly save the day to us.
>
> U.S. Grant.

If this was no sign of distrust, what could be more so than his proving his faith by his works, and abandoning the field as lost till Buell in person came up at 1 p. m.? Sherman's chivalric conduct is all the merest fiction. His own report, as above stated, and his retiring on Snake-creek bridge, by which he could have escaped to the river below, proves his cautious, and perhaps correct, intent to save himself and what troops he could on the expected capture of the landing he made no effort to prevent. He made no more use of the brigade sent him by McClernand to support his left than Grant did of Buell's division reaching Savannah at noon on the 5th, by means of which the Confederates could have been driven back without the necessary loss of a single Union soldier.

This warning against Halleck is proven clearly right by the intrigue developed at the head of this prefatorial chapter; and his statement, on which rests everything that could ever be claimed for Sherman, is as purely a fiction as that of "Jack the Giant Killer," or the Greek legend of "Ixion and the Cloud," and his report proves it such. Never was the truth more clearly established than by him (Halleck) that the "evil that men do lives after them; the good dies mostly with themselves." If he ever did the country a real service during the war, it stands upon the Popish dogma that "whatever is, is right;" and the Latin aphorism of "*de mortuis nil nisi bonum*" was never more entirely than in his case proven "more worthy in the breach than the observance." That the dead should, of course, or in any case, stand in the way of the life, of truth, or of justice, to living men or measures, is. as great an absurdity as the mourning of the Spartans at each darkness of the moon, which religiously kept them away from Marathon when the lights and liberties of Greece itself were about to be extinguished by the still existing darkness and superstition of the Asiatic world.

And here, lest it be forgotten, this compiler of fictions, exploded like percussion caps against the truth, to their own extinction, declares his intention, that in each and every chapter of this commentary he will endeavour to impress upon the reader, weary or otherwise of repetition, that—

1st. About the only truth worthy of record in the reports of these great commanders is that Buell saved the army at 5 p. m., which Grant and Sherman retired from, and gave up as lost at 10 to 12 a.m., April 6, 1862.

2nd. That if ever, as Whitelaw Reid intimates, a defeat was organized, it was done at Shiloh.

3rd. That Buell's army was purposely kept back during three days of perpetually expected attack at Shiloh.

4th. That the troops of Buell at hand on the 5th of April might have defeated the enemy, if they had not been purposely rejected; and this would have been done without the loss of a single Union soldier.

5th. That the otherwise inexplicable events of the Shiloh campaign can only be accounted for from January to June, 1862, by a systematic effort to protract the war, as had been agreed by the war cabal at Washington.

6th. That Grant, Sherman, and Halleck could have, on this theory alone, obtained not only impunity but reward for the. slaughter and disgrace of Shiloh, and other otherwise unaccountable events of the war, the most direct evidence being the choice of Halleck instead of Buell, March 11, 1862, to control the war in the West, when the capture of Florence and the upper Tennessee was the great direct measure to be done or not on the 11th of March, 1862. If there is any other explicable theory of the protraction of the war than by the failure to take possession of the upper Tennessee after the fall of Fort Henry, let the writer of this digressive treatise go into disgrace here and hereafter.

After looking over, for a while, in the national library, the numerous fallacies and fictions as to the Shiloh campaign, this compiler had at last concluded to disperse them by a commentary on the histories of Badeau and Bowman. He had not half his work done when his proposed 150 pages were exhausted, and he had scarcely a fact *per se* to show, except the fact of fallacies extinguished generally by each other.

He, however, by looking over official documents, and comparing them with his own, found that about all that had been said or done by the chief actors in the campaign must have been done by the authority of some power in Washington delegated by the Government, which the Government did not publicly acknowledge or avow.

It was plain that blundering and incapacity, even on a battle-field, were not considered censurable, when the object of the junto in Washington was advanced without too much risk of exposure and ultimate defeat. Violations of the army regulations, of the articles of war, or of the established laws of military art and science, of the grossest character, which subserved the purposes of the party in power, were considered meritorious rather than otherwise.

This state of affairs had often been charged during the war and since, but no very specific evidence was adduced to establish the charge.

Immediately on the capture of Fort Henry, when the way was opened up to Florence, Alabama, the question at once arose, whether the war should be virtually ended by the occupation of the upper Tennessee and the capture of Chattanooga, or should be continued a year or more by delaying such occupation, which could have been effected with little time, risk, or expense then. As will be seen, Buell had been urging this as far as military propriety would allow. He was sustained by McClellan, who, about March 1, 1862, wrote Halleck that it was important to seize Decatur, Alabama; and he should have ordered it.

The question first to be settled was the seizure of Florence, near the Charleston and Memphis Railroad, so as to prevent A. Sidney Johnson joining Bragg and Beauregard at Corinth.

The matter was, of course, discussed in the Cabinet, but was doubtless settled by the congressional cabal or committee on the war, or over and under the war, more properly called. It was nothing but a mask to cover the cabal. The decision not to take and fortify Florence was the decision to give Halleck the control of the war on the Tennessee instead of Buell: to leave the road past Florence open, and to protract the war, which was done, against Buell's urgency. It then became a work of supererogation for the writer to enter upon any specific examination into the character or conduct of the commanders intrusted with the prolongation of the war

Their true character as military jobbers in bloodshed, and not leaders, was settled at once. They were under a contract or obligation to extend the war, instead of ending it for a consideration, of course. And while no honourable soldier would go into such an undertaking for any earthly consideration, these officers understood that they were to have all that was to be had in their line if the speculation succeeded.

It did succeed, and they have had and now enjoy their purchased positions and perquisites. This bargain was doubtless consummated when Grant went up to St. Louis the last week in January, 1862, to see Halleck, Sherman being there; and this was doubtless the initiation of the Tennessee and Cumberland expeditions, referred to in Sherman's speech at St. Louis in 1865. In this speech he gave Halleck the credit of these expeditions, and asserted the reverse of the fact, that Halleck, but for delays occasioned by Buell would have gone on to Florence, instead of stopping at Savannah, or rather Pittsburgh.

This bargain or arrangement once understood, everything about the battle and campaign of Shiloh is made plain. This shows why the expedition was started from Paducah without proper forage, ammunition, proper stores, or intrenching tools, such as it should have had.

This accounts for taking along the sick, purposely to incumber the camps with hospitals, for the feigning on Eastport, for the condition of the roads out from the landing to Shiloh, for the scattering of the camps, for taking a position commanded by high ground in front, with a bushy screen for the enemy. It accounts for the failure to order entrenchments, and the refusal of tools to strengthen the front. A battle was invited without regard to any other result. That a defeat was at first intended to be organized admits not of a doubt by those who understand the rules of war.

The expectation of Sherman and Grant of an attack on on the 3rd of April; the effort to keep Buell back till the 7th and 8th, or till after the fight; the rejection of his troops when they came three days to five days before they were wanted, while the enemy in front was estimated at one hundred thousand men; the indifference of Grant on and off the field; his lingering at the landing and on his boat; Sherman's recklessness on the battlefield and the turning over of his last-organized troops to his aids at 9 to 10 a. m. all point to an intended defeat, or a carelessness for the result, without apprehension of reprimand from Washington. And they got no such reprimand; they got reward and promotion.

Then the refusal of Halleck to make any investigation, though unanimously demanded after the battle, except by the cowards and skulkers; the silence of the junto in Washington, so sharp after McClellan; Halleck's statement, with an audacity without parallel, that Sherman had saved the day he had done most to lose; the delay at Shiloh after the battle; the snail pace to Corinth, all to throw away time; the suspension of all operations in Western Tennessee, which let Bragg loose after Buell; the purposely mismanaged campaign in Virginia; Bragg's raid into Kentucky; and the displacement of Buell all point to a power at Washington that had determined to protract the war.

Besides this, the promotion of Sherman on the capture of Corinth, for misconduct at Shiloh, and the translation of Halleck to Washington as Commander-in-Chief Halleck, who had laid the foundation of all this delay, and disaster, and bloodshed, by the refusal to occupy Florence all told the same story.

And the story was, that the object was to make use of the war to carry the elections of 1864, which was done done at an expense of blood and money past estimation; at the risk of national calamity too terrible for contemplation; and was the commission of a crime by their own Government against the army and the country without a parallel in the annals of the world. And here all explanation or exposition of the Shiloh campaign might terminate with this preface, but the book is written and partly paid for.

The character of the instrument employed by the Washington junto as the principal in this enormous intrigue may here appropriately be given by himself.

His untimely death is a calamity to this writer, and to the ends of justice, as he is beyond the reach of human law or even human execration. To deceive Buell, to humbug the people, and cover the intrigue was the question: and here is the way he did it, or had it done:

Halleck to the War Office at Washington.
St. Louis, March 3, 1862.
Grant has left his command and gone to Nashville without my authority. I can get no returns or reports from him; I am worn out and tired with this negligence and inefficiency. (*Second act of the juggle.*)

Halleck to Grant.

March 4th, 1862.

You will place Major General C. F. Smith in command of the expedition (up the Tennessee) and remain yourself at Fort Henry. Why don't you obey my orders? &c., &c. (*Third act of the juggle.*)

Halleck at St. Louis to Buell at Nashville, Tennessee.

March 4th, 1862.

Grant, with all available force, has gone up the Tennessee river to break the road at Humboldt, &c. (*First act of the juggle.*)

The object of all this was understood by all the parties concerned, except Buell and Smith; Sherman being as it were the audience and claquer all to himself and. for himself.

Buell may have been deceived, and thought the expedition was bound for Florence. It did not, however, leave Fort Henry till the 10th; got to Savannah on the 11th; then, presto, as the jugglers say, and Grant was in command again on the 13th March, as he writes Smith on the 11th. (*Last act of the juggle.*) The expedition was long enough under command of Smith to give colour to his location of the Shiloh battlefield. This had been doubtless arranged at St. Louis. Sherman's Bowman says that Halleck ordered the position on the west side of the river, to prevent Beauregard joining Johnson at Decatur.[3] (*To keep up the juggle this is written, but lets it out.*)

This character of Halleck is enough to settle the characters

---

3. This needs no explanation to a close or military reader, but may to others. Buell's effort was to prevent Johnson going from Decatur to Corinth by railroad. Halleck's effort had been to get Johnson to Corinth, past Florence, from Decatur; but here Sherman says, that the effort was to prevent Beauregard joining Johnson at Decatur, (an absurdity,) and, therefore, it was necessary to locate the army on the west side of the river, which is a double fiction, or worse. To take and hold Florence was to prevent the junction of the rebel armies, and for this purpose Florence itself, on the north or east bank, was the point to reach. Sherman avoids this truth, for the purpose of deception, in one case, as to the true object in view by Buell, which is one fiction, and makes a statement against the fact to justify the location at Shiloh, where a battle could be invited, as it was to prolong the war, and this makes the double fiction. W. P. G.

of his coadjutors, Grant and Sherman; and it is easily shown, as are the eclipses of the almanac maker, or the programme of the travelling juggler, by the after-conduct of these men, that they were chosen to carry out the plan of protracting the war, for the reason that Halleck was a man that never advised a battle, never went near a skirmish on the Corinth approach, and kept his quarters out of reach of the heaviest artillery.

Grant could not or did not give an intelligent order, or perform a tactical manoeuvre on the battlefield of Shiloh, or any other battlefield, of himself, during the war. Sherman, at Shiloh, ruined everything he handled or meddled with in person on the field of Shiloh, and everywhere else. These were the men, and exceedingly proper men, chosen by the Aulic council at Washington to protract the war in 1862, and let it run according to political circumstances thereafter, till 1864 and 1865.

This commentator, then, with such characters to handle, claims and proclaims it his duty, as a truthful narrator, a soldier, and an honest man, to put the very worst possible construction upon the writings, words, and doings of these men. By their conduct since the war, they have rendered themselves subject to an indictment for false pretences, if nothing worse, in appropriating laurels they never won, in assuming merit they never had, and in claiming the gratitude of the people for having been the mere tools of political practitioners, to call them nothing worse.

They have been hired and paid for unnecessary bloodshed, for accumulating hundreds of millions of national debt, and for being the ministers of party frauds, and abuses without historical parallel. Are such hirelings fit to be trusted? If not hirelings, let their admirers tell us what they are, unless, like cunning stewards, they have become the owners of the estate, and will, if they can, by themselves or their successors, hold it in perpetuity, if not foiled in the impending attempt at the continuance of a corrupt administration of the Government of the Republic. Such, after as full an examination as possible of what chance records of the war are left, is the entire conviction of a West Point Graduate.

Washington, April 6, 1862.

Headquarters Fifth Division,
Camp Shiloh, April 18, 1862.

Captain J. A. Rawlins,
Assistant Adjutant General to General Grant:

Sir: I had the honour to report that on Friday, the 4th instant, the enemy's cavalry drove in our pickets, posted about a mile and a half in advance of my centre, on the main Corinth road, capturing one first lieutenant and seven men; that I caused a pursuit by the cavalry of my division, driving them back about five miles, killing many. On Saturday the enemy's cavalry was again very bold, coming well down to our front; yet I did not believe he designed anything but a strong demonstration. On Sunday morning early, the 6th instant, the enemy drove our advance guard back on the main body, when I ordered under arms all my division, and sent word to General McClernand, asking him to support my left; to General Prentiss, giving him notice that the enemy was in our front in force; and to General Hurlbut, asking him to support General Prentiss. At that time, 7 a. m., my division was arranged as follows:

1st Brigade. Composed of 6th Iowa, Col. J. A. McDowell; 40th Illinois, Col. Hicks; 46th Ohio, Col. Worthington; and the Morton Battery on the extreme right, guarding the bridge on the Purdy road, over Owl creek.

2nd Brigade. Composed of 5th Illinois, Col. D. Stuart; 54th Ohio, Col. T. Kilby Smith; 71st Ohio, Col. Mason; on the extreme left, guarding the ford over Lick creek.

3rd Brigade. Composed of 77th Ohio, Col. Hildebrand; 53rd Ohio, Col. Appler; 57th Ohio, Col. Munger; on the left of the Corinth road, its right resting on Shiloh meeting-house.

4th Brigade. Composed of 72nd Ohio, Col. Buckland; 48th Ohio, Col. Sullivan; 7th Ohio, Col. Cockerill; on the right of the Corinth road, its left resting on Shiloh meeting-house.

Two batteries of artillery—Taylor's and Waterhouse's—were posted, the former at Shiloh and latter on a bridge to the left, with a front fire over open ground, between Monger's and Appler's regiments. The cavalry and companies of the Fourth Illinois, under Colonel Dickey, were posted in a large open field to the left and rear of Shiloh meeting-house, which I regard as the centre of my position.

Shortly after 7 a. m., with my entire staff, I rode along a portion of our front, and when in the open field before Appler's regiment, the enemy's pickets opened a brisk fire on my party, killing my orderly, Thomas D. Holliday, of Company H, Second Illinois cavalry. The fire came from the bushes, which line a small stream that rises in the field in front of Appler's camp, and flows to the north along my whole front.

This valley afforded the enemy a partial cover, but our men were so posted as to have a good fire at him as he crossed the valley and ascended the rising ground on our side. About 8 a. m. I saw the glistening bayonets of heavy masses of infantry to our left front, in the woods beyond the small stream alluded to, and became satisfied, for the first time, that the enemy designed a determined attack on our whole camp. All the regiments of my division were then in line of battle, at their proper posts. I rode to Colonel Appler and ordered him to hold his ground at all hazards, as he held the left flank of our first line of battle, and I informed him that he had a good battery on his right, and strong supporters to his rear. General McClernand had promptly and energetically responded to my request, and had sent me three regiments, which were posted to protect Waterhouse's battery and the left flank of my line.

The First Day

The battle began by the enemy opening a battery in the woods to our front, and throwing shell into our camp. Taylor's and Waterhouse's batteries promptly responded, and I then observed heavy battalions of infantry passing obliquely to the left across the open field in Appler's front; also other columns advancing directly upon my division.

Our infantry and artillery opened along the whole line, and the battle became general. Other heavy masses of the enemy's forces kept passing across the field to our left, and directing their course on General Prentiss's. I saw at once that the enemy designed to pass my left flank, and fall upon Generals McClernand and Prentiss, whose line of camps was almost parallel with the Tennessee river, and about two miles back from it. Very soon the sound of musketry and artillery announced that Prentiss was engaged, and about 9 a. m. I judged that he was falling back. About this time Appler's regiment broke in disorder, followed by Mungen's regiment, and the enemy pressed forward on Waterhouse's battery, thereby exposed.

The three Illinois regiments in immediate support of the battery stood for some time, but the enemy's advance was so vigorous, and the fire so severe, that when Colonel Raith, of the Forty-third Illinois, received a severe wound and fell from his horse, his regiment and the others manifested disorder, and the enemy got possession of three guns of this (Waterhouse's) battery.

Although our left was thus turned, and the enemy was pressing our whole line, I deemed Shiloh so important that I remained by it, and renewed my orders to Colonels McDowell and Buckland to hold their ground, and we did hold these positions until about 10 o'clock a. m., when the enemy had got his artillery to the rear of the left flank, and some change became absolutely necessary. Two regiments of Hildebrand's brigade Appler's and Mungen's had already disappeared to the rear, and Hildebrand's own regiment was in disorder. I therefore gave orders for Taylor's battery, still at Shiloh, to fall back as far as the Purdy and Hamburgh road, and for McDonald and Buckland to adopt that road as their new line.

I rode across the angle and met Behr's battery at the cross roads, and ordered it immediately to come into battery action right. Captain Behr gave the order, but he was almost immediately shot from his horse, when drivers and gunners fled in disorder, carrying off the caissons, and abandoning five out of the six guns without firing a shot. The enemy pressed on after gaining this battery, and we were again forced to choose a line of defence. Hildebrand's brigade had substantially disappeared from the field, though he himself bravely remained. McDowell's and Buckland's brigades still maintained their organizations, and were conducted by my aids so as to join on McClernand's right, thus abandoning my original camps and line.

This was about 10 30 a. m., at which time the enemy had made a furious attack on General McClernand's whole front. He struggled most determinedly, but finding him pressed, I moved McDowell's brigade directly against the left flank of the enemy, forced him back some distance, and then directed the men to avail themselves of every cover trees, fallen timber, and a wooded valley to our right; we held this position for four long hours, sometimes gaining and at others losing ground, General McClernand and myself acting in perfect concert and struggling to maintain this line.

While we were so hardly pressed, two Iowa regiments approached from the rear, but could .not be brought up to the severe fire that was raging in our front; and General Grant, who visited us on that ground, will remember our situation about 3 p. m. But about 4 p. m. it was evident that Hurlbut's line had been driven back to the river; and knowing that General Wallace was coming with reinforcements from Crump's Landing, General McClernand and I, on consultation, selected a new line of defence, with its right covering a bridge by which General Wallace had to approach.

We fell back as well as we could, gathering, in addition to our own, such scattered forces as we could find, and formed the line. During this change the enemy's cavalry charged us, but were handsomely repulsed by an Illinois regiment, whose number I did not learn at that time or since. The Fifth Ohio cavalry, which had come up, rendered good service in holding the enemy in check for some time, and Major Taylor also came up with a new battery, and got into position to get a good flank fire upon the enemy's column as he pressed on General McClernand's right, checking his advance; when General McClernand's division made a fine charge on the enemy, and drove him back into the ravines to our front and right. I had a clear field about two hundred yards wide in my immediate front, and contented myself with keeping the enemy's infantry at that distance during the rest of the day.

Colonel J. A. McDowell, commanding the first brigade, held his ground all Sunday, till I ordered him to fall back, which he did in line of battle, and, when ordered, he conducted the attack on the enemy's left in good style. In falling back to the next position he was thrown from his horse and injured, and his brigade was not in position on Monday morning. His subordinates, Colonels Hicks and Worthington, displayed great personal courage. Colonel Hicks led his regiment in the attack on Sunday, and received a wound winch it is feared may prove mortal. He is a brave and gallant gentleman, and deserves well of his country. Lieutenant Colonel Walcott, of the Forty-sixth Ohio, was severely wounded on Sunday, and has been disabled ever since.

My division was made up of regiments perfectly new, nearly all having received their muskets for the first time at Paducah. None of them had been under fire, or beheld heavy columns of an enemy bearing down on them, as they did on last Sunday. To expect of them the coolness and steadiness of older troops would be wrong. They knew not the value of combination and organization; when individual fear seized them, the first impulse was to get away.

My third brigade did break much too soon, and I am not yet advised where they were Sunday afternoon and Monday morning.

LIST OF KILLED AND WOUNDED.

First brigade.

	Killed		Wounded		Missing	
	Officers	Men	Officers	Men	Officers	Men
6th Iowa Vols.						
	2	49	3	217	0	39
40th Ill. ,,						
	1	42	7	148	0	2

46th Ohio „					
2	32	3	147	0	52

Second brigade.

55th Ill. „					
1	45	8	183	0	41
54th Ohio „					
2	22	5	128	0	32
71st „					
1	12	0	52	0	45

Third brigade.

77th Ohio „					
1	48	7	107	0	53
57th „					
2	7	0	82	0	33
53rd „					
0	7	0	39	0	5

Fourth brigade.

72nd Ohio „					
2	13	5	85	0	49
48th „					
1	13	3	70	1	45
70th „					
0	9	1	53	1	39

Taylor's battery, no report.

Behr's „					
1	0	0	0	0	0
Barrett's „					
0	1	0	5	0	0
Waterhouse's do.					
0	1	3	14	0	0
Orderly Holliday					
1					
—	—	—	—	—	—
16	302	45	1230	6	435

Killed, wounded, &c.

Officers killed   16

    „   wounded   45

    „   missing   6

Soldiers killed 302x261–563, killed

    „   wounded   1230

    „   died since the battle   261

    „   missing   435

Aggregate loss, 2,034 in the division.

The enemy captured seven of our guns on Sunday, but on Monday we recovered seven, not the identical guns we had lost, but enough in number to. balance the account. At the time of recovering our camps our men were so fatigued that we could not follow the retreating masses of the enemy, but on the following day I followed up with Buckland's and Hildebrand's brigades for six miles, the results of which I have already reported.

The cavalry of my command kept to the rear, and took little part in the action; but it would have been madness to have exposed horses to the musketry fire under which we were compelled to remain from Sunday at 8 a. m. till Monday at 4 p. m.

W. T. Sherman,
Brevet Gen. Com. 5th Div.

Extract from Bowman's *Sherman and His Campaign*.

The enemy's forces under General A. S. Johnston, consisting of the corps of Polk, Bragg, and Hardee, of two divisions each, and the reserve division of Brigadier General Breckinridge, having successively evacuated Columbus and Nashville, and abandoned Tennessee and Kentucky, with the exception of Memphis and Cumberland Gap, had concentrated at Corinth, in Mississippi, and were there awaiting the development of our plans, ready to act, according to circumstances, on the offensive or defensive, and to take advantage of any error we might make. The position was well chosen for observing our movements, for covering the line of the Mississippi, or for menacing the flank and rear of an army invading Mississippi and Alabama.

General Halleck decided to advance up the Tennessee river as far as practicable by water, then to debark on the west bank, attack the enemy at Corinth, and endeavour to cut him off from the east, and compel his surrender, either at Corinth or on the banks of the Mississippi. Grant was ordered to move up the Tennessee, and Buell to march from Nashville and join him near Savannah, Tennessee.

On the 14th of March Sherman, with the leading division of Grant's army, passed up the Tennessee on transports, and after making a feint of landing at Eastport, dropped down the stream and disembarked at Pittsburgh Landing. It was Sherman's intention to march from this point seven miles, in the direction of Iuka, and then, halting his infantry, to dispatch the cavalry to the nearest point on the Memphis and Charleston railway. The attempt was made, but the enemy was encountered in greater force than had been expected, and it did not succeed.

In the meanwhile, Major General Charles F. Smith, who had command of the advance, having landed his own second division at Savannah, had selected Pittsburgh Landing as the most favourable position for the encampment of the main body of the army, and under his instructions Sherman and Hurlbut, who, with the fourth division, had closely followed him, went into camp there. In the course of a few days they were joined by the first and sixth divisions of McClernand and Prentiss, and by Smith's own division from Savannah; and Major General Grant himself arrived and took command in person.

During the last week of March the Army of the Tennessee only waited for the Army of the Ohio. General Buell had informed General Grant that he would join him before that time; but he had encountered great delays, and on the morning of the 6th of April the Army of the Ohio had not yet come. It was hourly expected. Instructions had been sent by General Grant to expedite its advance, and to push on to Pittsburgh. The importance of the crisis was apparent, for Johnston would naturally seek to strike Grant before Buell's arrival: but Buell marched his troops with the same deliberation as if no other army depended upon his promptness, By express orders, he even caused intervals of six miles to be observed between his divisions on the march, thus lengthening out his column to a distance of over thirty miles.

Extracts from General Grant's report of Shiloh.

Headquarters District West Tennessee,
Pittsburgh, April 9, 1862.

To Captain N. H. McLean, &c.:

It becomes my duty again to report another battle, fought between two great armies, one contending for the best Government to be desired, and the other for its destruction. It is pleasant to record the success of the army contending for the former principle.

On Sunday morning our pickets were attacked and driven in by the enemy. The battle waxed warm on the left and centre, ranging at times to all parts of the line. There was the most continuous firing of musketry and artillery ever heard on this continent kept up till nightfall.

The enemy having forced the centre line to fall back nearly half way from their camps to the landing, at a late hour in the afternoon a desperate effort was made by the enemy to turn our left and get possession of the landing, transports, &c. This point was guarded by the gunboats *Tyler* and *Lexington*, Captains Gwin and Shirk commanding, with four 24-pound Parrot guns and a battery of rifled guns. As there is a deep and impassable ravine for artillery and cavalry, and very difficult for infantry, at this point, no troops were stationed there, except the necessary artillerists and a small infantry force for their support.

Just at this moment the advance of Major General Buell's column, part of the division of General Nelson, arrived. The two generals named both being present, an advance was immediately made upon the point of attack, and the enemy was soon driven back.

In this repulse much is due to the presence of the gunboats *Tyler* and *Lexington* and their able commanders, Captains Gwin and Shirk. During the night the divisions under Generals Crittenden and McCook arrived. General Lew. Wallace, at Crump's landing, six miles below, was ordered, at an early hour in the morning, to hold his division in readiness to move in any direction he might be ordered. At 11 o'clock a. m. the order was delivered to move it up to Pittsburgh, but, owing to its being led by a circuitous route, did not arrive in time to take part in Sunday's action.

My force was too much fatigued, from two days' hard fighting and exposure in the open air to a drenching rain during the intervening night, to pursue immediately. Night closed in with a heavy rain, making the woods impassable for artillery next morning. General Sherman, however, followed the enemy, finding that the main part of their army had retreated in good order," &c.

I feel it a duty, however, to a gallant and able officer Brigadier General W. T. Sherman to make special mention. He not only was with his command the entire two days of the action, but displayed great judgement and skill in the management of his men. Although severely wounded in the hand on the first day, his place was never vacant. He was again wounded, and had three horses shot under him, &c.

Lieutenant Colonel McPherson, attached to my staff as chief of engineers, deserves more than a passing notice for his activity and courage. All the ground around our camps has been reconnoitered by him, and the plans, carefully prepared under his supervision, give the most accurate information of the nature of the approaches to our lines. During the two days' battle he was constantly in the saddle, leading the troops as they arrived to points where their services were required. During the engagement he had a horse shot under him. At present I can only give our loss approximately at 1,500 killed and 3,500 wounded; 200 horses were killed.

U. S. Grant.

CHAPTER 1

Intoductory

The south today is more formidable and arrogant than she was two years ago, and we lose far more by having an insufficient number of men than from any other cause. We are forced to invade; we must keep the war South. They are not only ruined and exhausted, but humbled in pride and spirit. (Sherman's letter after Vicksburg.)

The enemy having forced the centre line to fall back nearly half way from the camp to the landing, at a late hour in the afternoon a desperate effort was made by the enemy to turn our left, and get possession of the landing, transports, &c.

This point was guarded by the gunboats *Tyler* and *Lexington*, Captains Gwin and Shirk, commanding, with four twenty-four pound guns and a battery of rifled guns. As there is a deep and impassable ravine for artillery and cavalry and very difficult for infantry, at this point, no troops were stationed there, except the necessary artillerists and a small infantry force for their support.

Just at this moment the advance Major General Buell's column, a part of the division of General Nelson arrived; the two generals named, both being present. An advance was immediately made upon the point of attack, and the enemy was soon driven back.

U. S. Grant.

Extract from General Grant's Letter to the Society of the

Army of the Tennessee.

Washington, April 7, 1871.

General W. W. Belknap.

Give my congratulations to the gallant Society of the Army of the Tennessee, &c. The battle of Shiloh, though much criticized at the time, will ever he remembered by those engaged in it as a 'brilliant success,' won with raw troops over a superior force, and under circumstances the most unfavourable to the Union troops.

U. S. Grant.

The writer of this treatise on the Shiloh campaign of 1862 claims nothing more than to be an imperfect compiler of facts, fallacies, and fictions, in regard to this extraordinarily understood and entirely misunderstood campaign. It stands forth now as a campaign more unexampled in its results, so far as they are known, than any this age or country has ever witnessed, in regard to its influence on the politics and policy of this so-called republic of the world.

This compiler will sometimes endeavour to rise to the grade of a narrator or relater of events and their bearing upon each other and upon parties or individuals well known to the people of the Union.

He cannot aspire to the dignity of a historian such as Headly or Hume, or Greeley or Gibbon, or Badeau or Bancroft, to close up the comparative alliteration. Abjuring everything in the shape of the philosophy of history, or historical philosophy, as to the meaning of which he professes his entire ignorance, he suggests the students of that science to Swinton or Schlagel, or Sherman's *Bowman*, or McCauley's *Niehbur*, or even to Ned Buntline himself, as having far more philosophical capacity, or at least audacity, or even veracity, than several of the above-suggested historians of the rebellion, and especially the historiographers of the Shiloh campaign now in question: Instance Badeau and Bowman. All he does claim in the line of Lindlay Murray is, that his syntax shall be as near the standard of the illustrious characters at the head of this chapter and of the army, and of the army and navy of the republic, as circumstances, and room, and time will permit.

And that his conclusions from the same premises shall be no wider apart than those of the chivalric Sherman, in the first quotation, and that there shall be few, if any, wider interjections between his premises and conclusions more difficult to span or fathom than the ravine for artillery and cavalry thrown in between the arrival of Buell and his rescue of Pittsburgh landing, &c., so luminously related by the illustrious President of the republic.

And, having thus introduced these august personages, which, for the present occupy and require, of choice or of necessity, so much of the attention of this treatise and this Union, an analysis, however imperfect, may next be undertaken to develop the profundity of Sherman, and extract from the martial and naval erudition of Grant the true meaning and intent of their respective paragraphs illustrating this chapter.

The condition of the South being in question, take from Sherman's paragraph all extraneous matter, and the solution will be perfect, as thus:

The South this moment is more formidable and arrogant than she was two years ago. She is not only ruined and exhausted, but broken in pride and spirit." There it is; how luminous, how like well; like Sherman, of course.

This is a favourite practice of antithesis habitual to this "great commander" who thus, in an unconsciously playful manner, seems only to express that he may expunge himself, as at the West Point black-board after a demonstration. This practice may be more readily observed in the chapters on "Sherman's Evidence and Cross-examination." These specimens of logic, or elements of evidence, may not be as profound or clear as "Starkie on Evidence," but will be found far more original, and infinitely more inconclusive, to which condition it seems his effort to reduce his own evidence in usual cases, even without a rebutter, of which there is seldom a necessity.

Next, to proceed with the illustrative paragraph of the illustrious President, with which it has been presumed to illuminate this straggling production, it should first be premised, in historical justice, that it contains, if less syntax, much more of conclusion, however extremely ultimate, than does the conclusive production of his admiring friend the general, &c. The solution, however, is a trifle more tedious, not to say abstruse, by reason of the depth and width and ponderosity, not to say prolixity, of the syntax to be developed, with more or less grammatical ability and mechanical skill. First steam out, with all possible regard and respect for Captains Gwin and Shirk, the gunboats *Tyler* and *Lexington*, these captains commanding, with four twenty-four Parrot guns and a battery of rifled guns, then filling up the ravine for artillery and cavalry, which last are thus made to play the patriotic part of the noble Curtius (or, perhaps, properly Curtis G. H. or Grant Harper's Curtis) in the pit of the Roman forum, some time since, letting, meantime, the hostile infantry, if any, stand from under, while packing or parking the artillerists nearer the landing; then marching off "the small infantry force" to swell Sherman's corporal's guard at the close of the battle, which, having no troops, as Greeley says, after 8 a. m., he must have need for; since Grant says, by his "personal efforts" like a steel-clad paladin of old, he saved the army.

Having, with so much time and strain, cleared off these traverses or interjections between the President's premises and conclusion, we do reach the fact, by no means seemingly intended to be expressed, if possibly to be avoided by this able rhetorician and commander, that "at a late hour in the afternoon a desperate effort was made to turn our left and get possession of the landing, transports," &c. (That is, trains, artillery, generals, and army.) "Just at this moment General Nelson, with the advance of Major General Buell's column, arrived, both Generals being present, when an advance was by these generals made, and the enemy driven back." Here is a necessarily handsome, but a hardly and niggardly wrung-out admission of almost providential aid in a desperate extremity, with not a word of acknowledgement, much less of gratitude, for deliverance from the very closing jaws of destruction. And then the matter is as indifferently dropped as the stump of a cigar. It is no wonder, then, that a mind so indifferent to benefits, and a memory so callous to their recollection, selfish, ungenerous, and unjust, should, with the weight of honours and emoluments thrust upon their possessor, utterly ignore such a service, after nine long years of enjoyment and prosperity, due alone to such a providential rescue April 6, 1862.

No wonder that their preservation from this very maelstrom of destruction should cultivate entire mental obliteration of the past, and the man, made what he is by the criminality of that day, should write such a letter as the above, claiming this deliverance from disgrace and destruction as a "brilliant success."

Yes, a "brilliant success" won by him over a superior force, while in command of the Army of the Tennessee at Pittsburgh Landing, April 6th, 1862.

Should any intelligent and impartial man, without knowing anything personally or historically of Grant or Sherman, have the above-quoted paragraphs referred to him, by which to judge of the characters and qualifications of their writers, he might justly conclude, that the writer of the first paragraph had not a very perfectly-balanced intellect, and the writer of the last might have serious imperfections of both head and heart. Such is the fact, such will be found the fact, from everything these distinguished personages have said or done or written, hereinafter stated or having reference, as a part of this compendium of the Shiloh campaign of 1862.

Taking a fair average of everything these men have ever said or done of themselves substantially, the above quotations are a fair criterion by which their degree of usefulness and capacity may be properly determined. They are the inevitable results of the system under which the war was carried on and carried through, and it is about time that the people, having some little interest in the welfare of the Union, should endeavor to establish their real value, before intrusting them any further with the administration of the military and civil Government of the Union.

The writer first proposed to develop the true history and character of these officers by a commentary upon their biographies, more especially that of Sherman, as the more obtrusive of the two, but he soon found himself in a maze of perpetual digression, as incomprehensible as the crudities and fallacies and fictions of Badeau and Bowman he undertook to explain and explode. The diary extracts hereinafter quoted constitute the earliest germ of this treatise. When written, the writer saw much that was out of rule not therein recorded. He first attempted, with thousands of others, to have an investigation, immediately after the battle, by order of General Halleck; but all were referred by him to Grant and Sherman, the officers whose conduct was to be investigated. Next he, with thousands of others, in and out of the army, applied to the Ohio Senators, Messrs. Sherman and Wade, the latter of whom was the head of the Committee on the Conduct of the War. No answer could be had from them, and this relator, having written to the Hon. Y. B. Horton, of Ohio, received an answer as follows:

Washington, June 6, 1862.
Dear Sir: Your letter of May 23 came. to hand. I saw Mr. Wade, as you requested. It is a delicate matter for any one connected with the legislative department of Government, to interfere with the military details, and I doubt whether Mr. Wade will think it judicious to do anything. Whatever is done in regard to inquiries, will have to be accomplished, I think, through the regular military channels.

Yours, truly,

V. B. Horton.

It was then plain to him that there was a power of some description at Washington, by which the architects of defeat and slaughter at Shiloh enjoyed perhaps something even more than impunity. It seemed a nonplus.

The French astronomer, Le Verrier, having noted the perturbation of Herschel, the planet, for which Saturn, his hither neighbour, could not be made accountable, betook himself to the laws of Newton, and perhaps Kepler, in reference to planetary or material gravitation, in the inverse ratio of the squares of the distances, and perhaps the description of heavenly bodies of equal areas in equal lines, on the plane of their orbit, and with little more science than is exercised by the butcher or the grocer with his steelyards and counter-scales in the weight of a pound of beef or butter, he discovered his new planet. Moral influences have more intricate laws, and are far more complex in the manner of their solution; but, by observing the seemingly reckless, but clearly designing, and calculating, and inviting manner in which Grant and Sherman had allowed their army to be attacked; the deliberate movements of Grant after the attack; the destructive performances of Sherman on the field; and winding up by the audacious fiction of Halleck, that Sherman had saved the "fortunes of a day" it was the unanimous conviction he had done most to lose. This relator was impressed with the conviction that Halleck had, in some way, an individual interest in the result of what had occurred at Shiloh.

The indisposition to make any investigation, and afterward the snail pace to Corinth, gave a solution to a conversation that had taken place in Halleck's tent a day or two after he reached Pittsburg. Sherman's conduct on the march to Corinth, in magnifying the difficulties and dangers encountered, and his congratulatory order after the capture of Corinth, in which Halleck and the tedious and more than tardy achievement of capturing Corinth were so extravagantly exalted, as about the most brilliant and important victory of history, next to Shiloh by Grant, of course; faintly suggested an idea of collusion somewhere. Some words used in Sherman's address, or report, as to the aridity of the region, &c., called to mind a reported talk, such as is before mentioned. And when Halleck went to Washington as commander-in-chief, in July, 1862, the inference was plain, that these commanders were in accord with each other and with some influences at Washington, overriding the articles of war. This then seemed a possible solution of disturbing influences behind and above military laws. The perturbation of Herschel, calculated by Le Verrier, outside of any attractions for which, as has been said, the chronic old Saturn could be brought to look—also hinted a clue. Hence the impunity to Grant for keeping Buell back to risk the loss of a battle, of which the writer was then ignorant. The promotion of Sherman, dating from the evacuation of Corinth, 26th May, and not from Shiloh, (too flagrant that,) was suggestive, in connection with his outside influences at Washington.

Extract from Sherman's official report of the siege of Corinth, dated at Corinth,

Mississippi. June, 1862.

It is a victory as important as any recorded in history. But a few days ago (two months) a large and powerful rebel army lay at Corinth, with outposts extending to our very camp at Shiloh. (*By special invitation, W. P. G.*) If with two such railroads as they possessed they could not supply their army with troops and stores, how can they attempt it in this poor, and, and exhausted part of the country?

The point here is, that Sherman writes as though the rebels had moved from a distance to where he was then and there at Corinth. These words are those which had been used by Halleck in saying that there should be no battle, as the "poor, arid, and exhausted state of the country" would compel an evacuation, &c., early in June, 1802. Sherman concludes by saying that success can only be accomplished by a ready and cheerful obedience to our leaders, (Halleck and Grant and he,) in whom we now (after the siege) have just reason for the most implicit confidence.

The letter of the Hon. V. B. Norten plainly proved that the Committee on the Conduct of the War was a cover, not an exposition, and might have been instituted to relieve the War Office of responsibility, which was the fact. Seeing no chance with the legislative or military authorities, plainly in collusion as to Shiloh, the writer became still more determined to hunt the matter down, as subversive of all justice or safety in the military, and all stability in the civil existence of the Government. He became determined, as desirous, to get at a solution, if possible, of this collusive conduct of the commanders in the field, and to find out how they were in accord with the influences at Washington.

Disgusted with a service in which incapacity, neglect, and cowardice, and worse were at a premium, even on a battlefield, he pursued a course not necessarily here exposed, by which he gained the court martial evidence detailed in a following chapter and never before made public. That he strove for the court martial is plain, from the following indorsement of General Sherman, on the letter of objections, for which see the end of this chapter:

> Respectfully forwarded.
> Colonel Worthington knew that the subject-matter of the charges were made by General Sherman, and placed in the hands of the judge advocate.
> He might have excepted to them before pleading, but he did not, but actually courted the trial and waived all objections on that point. The original proceedings[1] were sent to the Adjutant General's office, Washington, D. C., before any order was made by me, and sent back with the indorsement of the Judge Advocate General[2] that they did not require the orders or approval of the President.
> Had Colonel Worthington excepted to his trial at the right time, *viz*, before pleading, his exception would have been good. But it is now too late, as he boastingly waived all objections and courted investigation. The original proceedings will sent to the War Department for record.
>
> W. T. Sherman,
Maj. Gen. Comd'g.

[No date, T. W.]

---

1. Not the fact.
2. Not the fact.

Headquarters Dist. West Tennessee,
Jackson, Tenn., October 18, 1862.
Respectfully forwarded to the Headquarters of the Army,
Washington, D.C.

U. S. Grant,
Maj. Gen.

The prisoner did not make objections before pleading, for fear they might be sustained, in which case he would not get the evidence he was after, outside of Sherman's evidence. Sherman, he felt sure, would betray his violent enmity, as he did. To insure his careless, reckless manner of expression and exposition, the prisoner employed no counsel, and for fear the court might demur to the extreme sentence insisted on by Sherman, he made no defence, except of his diary extracts, or rather a statement to show that all and far more than therein charged was true. He had not foreseen that all evidence as to everything happening during the battle would be ruled out.

That audacity was not provided for. But he perfectly understands it now. It arose from Sherman's impunity for any act of his or his court, however criminal or unlawful, which would carry out the policy of those by whom the officers in question were employed to prolong the war. Knowing this then, August, 1862, he , might not have called the court. Such evidence was excluded, Because of its damning character, bearing on Grant, and especially on Sherman. It would, of course, have upset Halleck's glaring and most infamous fiction as to the conduct of Sherman at Shiloh. But in the light of subsequent events even that evidence would have had no effect upon the court, as it will not now likely have upon the general public; and this is another fearful result of promoting men for acts which, by the articles of war, or by common law, would disgrace or execute them by a sergeant's platoon.

The prisoner was indeed willing to waive a record so disgraceful to a West Point Graduate, and did not insist on the evidence, as Sherman's own report offered sufficient evidence to show how worse than worthless on the battlefield this witness, prosecutor, and court, all in one, had been. The prisoner did not then know that this incapacity, or worse, had gained him not only his promotion at Washington, but a lease of his position for the war. The record states, that the prisoner asked and was allowed counsel, but the fact was, that he asked only that one of his captains (Alexander) might assist in keeping the record, which was not allowed long, as soon after he was ordered on duty with the regiment in Memphis. And here may as well be made a digression as to another charge which came before the court, arising as follows:

About the 25th June, 1862, the colonel of the 40th Ohio, with 302 men for duty, no cavalry, and two light guns, had been left for capture at La Fayette, Tennessee, there being a force of 1,000 to 1,600 of the enemy, with headquarters not far southwest. He, however, soon finding out the danger through his pickets, at once fortified himself by the only closed field-work, constructed during the campaign. Grant, then at Memphis, had refused to allow the troops of this regiment their daily rations of whiskey, when on this fatigue duty, as had been allowed by Halleck, to break the monotony of the Corinthian advance of half a mile a day. He, Colonel W., was notified by Sherman, at Moscow, Tennessee, July 16, to join his brigade next day, (17th,) as he did when the brigade came up.

At the request of all hands who had built the fort, he allowed his sutler to bring up a few thousand rations of cherry-bounce, &c., from Memphis, thirty miles off. The division coming up on the 18th of July, the troops having been separated on detached service for some weeks, there were congratulations to the 46th Ohio for its escape from capture by means of its defences, and also convivialities, in which the colonel of the 46th Ohio was joined, of course, but attended to his usual duty in remaining behind to see that everything was got off in proper order, and nothing left behind.

The fort was evacuated at 8 a. m., and General Sherman, coming in to see the work at 10 a. m., noticed the colonel in a better humour, perhaps, than usual, as he wished and intended to be, and thus avoid giving his general of division his opinion as to his desertion of his first brigade at Shiloh, and exposure of the regiment without a horseman at La Fayette. It will be understood that the colonel of the 46th had been relieved from his command the day before, and the fort had been evacuated two hours before Sherman came in. On the strength of this affair, however, and the diary extracts, Sherman preferred a charge of "drunkenness on duty", as commander of the fort, from which the colonel had been relieved by special order the day before.[3]

He not only made this charge, but swore to the truth of this fiction, which he required his staff and several suborned witnesses to do also, and of course the prisoner was found guilty of being in command of a deserted post! Another necessary result of protractive policy.

The above properly belongs to the development of Sherman's character as a man of justice and veracity. It also illustrates the objects and requirements of the Washington cabal, who employed such instruments to carry on or carry back the war, as the policy of the party in power seemed to require.

The colonel of 46th Ohio has long and vainly endeavoured to have the incidents of the Shiloh campaign investigated by the Senate, or his court martial reported on by a committee of the House in Congress. It is now plain how useless was the endeavor. Such an investigation would develop much about the doings and misdoings of this inside ring and hidden cabinet council of the ruling party at Washington. It would disclose the price paid for procrastinating the war in the early winter of 1862, and the

---

3. Headquarters, Moscow, Tenn.,
July 16, 1862.
Colonel Worthington,
Commanding La Fayette.
Sir: We are ordered to move. My division will come tomorrow or the day after to La Fayette, where you will be prepared to join your brigade with all your men and means of transportation. "Be prepared to destroy your works then, and everything that would be of service to the enemy who may come in. We are to operate farther South. If Colonel McDowell be at La Fayette, or near there, please communicate to him this fact, and that he need not return to his camp here, but await our arrival at La Fayette.   W. T. Sherman, Maj. Gen.

55

price promised for the slaughter and disgrace of Shiloh, notwithstanding the extent and nature of the official documents suppressed and destroyed, and would prove the fact of this suppression and destruction. By this court martial is proven the suppression of what occurred at Shiloh, the day and night before the battle of Shiloh, April 6, 1862.

Through this necessarily digressive, and, in some sort, aggressive, treatise, this relator makes his appeal to the great court of last resort, the people of the Union, and more especially the volunteers of the rebellion, whose lives and hopes, and limbs, and health, and fortunes, were made subservient to the purposes of cowardly and scheming politicians, on and off the battlefields of the war.

Is there a man of character, who was in that service, who would have budged an inch towards a field of slaughter, where his general was employed to lose a battle, as a jockey is hired to lose a race?

To you who so cheerfully strained yourselves to furnish the sinews of the war against the rebellion—you, the people, who, in the path of duty to the republic, strove so faithfully and trustingly—to you, the people, is made this appeal—to you who risked your lives in camps and hospitals North and South, exposed your lives and limbs and blood upon the battle-fields of the Union for the Union, this appeal is made.

And while this appeal for justice is put forth, a solution is offered of the tangled mystery which for ten years has clouded the battlefield of Shiloh, and the incidents of that campaign. These incidents were clearly and directly connected with the great crisis of the war. That crisis clearly came with the determination of the Government at Washington to take no decisive advantage of the Tennessee river, in the winter of 1861-'62, to open a highway to the heart of the Confederacy. From December to March, the question of moving troops up the Tennessee to the Muscle shoals had been skillfully avoided by Halleck, and he had repeatedly declined a personal interview with Buell, to arrange as to this most important measure. A great parade had been made as to breaking up the railroads at Corinth, Jackson, and Humboldt, requiring land marches of from twenty to sixty miles, while the main connecting point at Florence, Alabama, was avoided, as will be seen, by Halleck. Let it then be established, that the occupation of Florence, and consequently of the Upper Tennessee valley, was purposely avoided, when so easily accomplished, with other studied neglect, tending to a prolongation of the war, and the intention of that prolongation is plain, and it is equally plain that it could only be for the political purpose of gaining the Presidential election.

What, had such a policy been known, or even suspected, would have been the results?

1. Volunteering would have been checked, and perhaps entirely suspended, and with such a policy to carry on the war by drafts would have been impossible.

2. The public credit would have been utterly prostrated.

3. The policy of anything like delay was a premium oil incompetence and neglect, if not cowardice itself.

4. It was a policy of bloodshed, to maintain a party more terrible and revolting, because more irresponsible, than the same policy to maintain a throne.

5. It required the payment or pensioning of those whose knowledge demanded pay for silence.

6. It gave impunity to official oppression and the acceptance of fictitious testimony, and the maintenance of trumped-up charges and consequent disgrace, or even death, to officers, for personal purposes, or who denounced the policy and its ministers. (See Colonel W's court-martial, the charges and the evidence.)

7. It led to the destruction or suppression of all true records of the war, and led to the retention of false reports for special purposes, of which there is ample evidence in this commentary.

8. Such a policy necessarily sanctioned and encouraged the violation of all established rules of war, as was the case at Shiloh, where every law of war possible was violated with impunity, and rewarded by promotion.

9. It abrogated all true criterion of military efficiency, and made that a merit which before had been a crime, punished by disgrace or death.

10. It was equivalent to the legalized extension of disease, and vice, and crime, the concomitants of war, indefinitely and without control.

11. Such a policy was actually the extension of aid and comfort to the enemy, as occurred in the failure to take Florence, or pursue, with ample means, the enemy after Shiloh.

12. Any established evidence of this policy must release the opposition to the war from any cause, from all odium arising from such opposition in 1862. While the war lasted, the sympathy of the people and the vote of the troops would most likely be as it was, on the side of the administration of the Government by the party responsible for the results of the war.

One result necessarily would be, that all possible means must betaken to conceal a policy so inhuman in its practice and terrible in its results. It led directly to a neglect of all reports from the field, and indeed of their suppression when made, as has to a great extent occurred. The writer is aware of one record of a court-martial entirely suppressed by General Sherman, as no doubt many such records have been by him, and especially by General Halleck, with the approval of General Grant.

The record of General Buell's court of inquiry, with the exception of the findings, cannot be had. The inquiry in Buell's case was not allowed to include the incidents preceding and during and immediately succeeding the. battle of Shiloh, proving, as did the suppression of these incidents on Colonel Worthington's trial, that they will not bear the light. It can be proven that the articles of the army regulations requiring division commanders to make immediate reports of all orders issued, was dispensed with, at least in the case of General Sherman. The orders issued by this general in his campaigns were, as a general rule, unknown at the War Office till the end of the war, when his order-books came in. These books are inaccessible, except by act of Congress, which cannot be had, and, if had, no order, the suppression of which was necessary to conceal the extension of the war policy could be found.

The institution of the Committee on the Conduct of the War for the ostensible purpose of instigating and keeping a record of its events, was a mere cover, against any investigation or history whatever, so that this terrible policy inaugurated the system of keeping no official records of the war, and suppressing those which were necessarily made. To conclude on this point, the writer feels assured that the members of this committee, with one or more members of the Cabinet, and two or more of the heads of the military bureaus, constituted, with the general-in-chief, Halleck, the Aulic council, which regulated the whole course of the war after 1861. These gentlemen in Congress were the Hons. B. F. Wade and Z. Chandler, with perhaps Yates and Sherman, of the Senate, and of course Cameron, wherever he was, and the Hons. Covode, Julian, and Gooch, of the House.

The Hon. Henry Wilson, chairman of the Committee on Military Affairs, must have been in some sort aware of the policy pursued.

This course must certainly have been repugnant to the principles and feelings of a man so honourable and benevolent; such a man as was Senator Henry Wilson, of Massachusetts,

As mild a mannered man
As ever cut a bore—or scuttled—

an amendment to an army bill.

Early in 1862 this relator made known to him that there was terrible neglect, or design, or worse, in the inauguration and consummation and consequences of the battle of Shiloh, and he thought he understood from him and others in the public councils that when the war was over its incidents of wrong and injustice would be righted, and all proper investigation had for its true history; but, as above suggested, this has been made impossible by its extension policy, and all or most official records of any consequence relative to the great rebellion will constitute no material part of future history.

If the statements hereinafter made, derived, as they are, from the official documents of the Shiloh campaign of 1862, and from the letters and biographies of Generals Grant, Sherman, Buell, and Ammen, including, of course, Colonel Worthington's court-martial record if these statements are established, and if the most prominent actors in this campaign (Halleck, Grant, and Sherman) acted on their own responsibility, that responsibility is shown to be such that, for its terrible and far-reaching results, they should be held responsible, whatever length of time has passed away. Otherwise they will continue to be, as they have been, the beneficiaries of their own wrong.

If they acted in obedience to the policy of the Government at Washington, in obedience to the will or advice of any man, or set of men, authorized to carry out that policy, they did so, as is plain upon the record, to the violation of all military law—all human justice.

It is a recognized principle, even by Napoleon, despot as he was, that no general is bound to expose his honour, or the honour or safety of his troops, to any policy or order of his Government at home. If he cannot obey without the violation of established military law, without risk to his soldiers' honour, and the welfare of his troops, he may resign, and avoid exposing both, as his duty it is to do.

If, then, these generals, in obedience to any power, legitimate or otherwise, at Washington, are guilty, as charged, with failing to take those measures urged by Buell to defeat the enemy, and close the war;—if at Shiloh the army was wilfully exposed, without guards or defences, to an invited attack; if an endeavor was made to keep reinforcements back which were needed for the safety of the Army of the Tennessee; if they refused to use sufficient of their forces at hand to defeat the enemy, with little or no loss to the Union army; if all this, and more, was done for the purpose of protracting the war, and if, in consequence of defeat, they were screened from punishment and rewarded with promotion, the case is clear, that they were bought up to serve a political purpose, for which they have been amply paid. But as buyers and sellers of misery and blood, and human life, and severed social and parental ties, and broken hearts, and blasted hopes, and ruined fortunes, all, and more than these, the dread concomitants of war, they have proved themselves unworthy of all human sympathy and public confidence in future, and subject to disgrace and punishment for the past.

Brennus, the barbarian Gaul, but threw his sword into the scale to swell the golden ransom for desolated Rome, in an age of barbarity and blood. But these statesmen, and these commanders, in this age of culture and refinement, have not hesitated to trade and truck and traffic for myriads upon myriads of lives and limbs, and rivers of blood and rivulets of tears, to satisfy a mad ambition for power and a grovelling greed of gain. If the charge is false, then let them answer, why was Buell, who would have pushed on the war, pushed out? Why was Halleck, who kept back the war, kept in? Why were these commanders, who organized defeat at Shiloh, and rejected the surest means of victory, promoted? Why were those who did the most to save the Army of the Tennessee from ruin and disgrace kept down and forced out of the military service? These questions are sufficient now. When satisfactorily answered, we may go into details as to how it is made a merit for commanders of the highest grade to give up their commands to subordinates, or give up the field as lost at noon of the day, and desert the ruin they had wrought.

Note.—   Letter of Objections.
                    Fort Pickering, September 17, 1862.
Adjutant General U. S. A.

Sir: I would most respectfully call your attention to the record on case of the trial of Colonel Thomas Worthington, 46th regiment O. V. I., by general court-martial, at Fort Pickering, Memphis, Tennessee, on the 14th August, 1862, and submit whether, from the evidence, it is not apparent that Major General Sherman is the accuser or prosecutor. It also appears manifest of record that the court was ordered by General Sherman. Is this not an irregularity, (see sec. 65, Article of War, act 29th May, 1830,) for which the record and proceedings should be set aside?

Very respectfully, your obedient servant,

T. Worthington,
Col. 46th Regt. O. V. I.

Indorsements on the above.

Headquarters 46th O. V. I.,
September 17, 1862.

Colonel Worthington asks that the proceedings of his court-martial may be examined and set aside.

Chas. C. Walcutt,
Lt. Col. Comd'g 46th O. V. I.

Headquarters 2nd Brig., 5th Div., Fort Pickering,
September 18, 1862.

Respectfully forwarded.   Jno. Adair McDowell,
Col. 6th Iowa Vols., 2nd Brig. Comd'g.

Respectfully forwarded.

Colonel Worthington knew that the subject-matter of the charges were made by General Sherman and placed in the hands of the judge advocate.

He might have excepted to them before pleading, but he did not, but actually courted the trial, and waived all objections on this point. The original proceedings[4] were sent to the Adjutant General's office, Washington, D.C., before any order was made by me, and sent back with the indorsement of the Judge Advocate General,[5] that they did not require the orders or approval of the President.

Had Colonel Worthington excepted to his trial at the right time, *viz*, before pleading, his exception would have been good. But it is now too late, as he boastingly waived all objections, and courted investigation. The original proceedings will be sent to the War Department for record.

W. T. Sherman,
Maj. Gen. Commanding.

[No date. T. W.]

---

4. Not the fact.
5. Not the fact.

Headquarters Dist. West Tennessee,
Jackson, Tenn., October 18, 1862.

Respectfully forwarded to the headquarters of the army, Washington, D.C.

U. S. Grant,
Maj. Gen.

Adjutant General's Office,
November 4, 1862.

Respectfully referred to the Judge Advocate General for report.

By order of the Secretary of War.
Thomas M. Vincent,
Ass't. Adj't. Gen.

Returned to the Adjutant General November 9. (See mem. within.)

The mem. within is as follows: (In pencil. T. W.)

Returned to the Adjutant General. The Secretary of War will direct what order shall be issued in this case..

C. P. Buckingham,
Brig Gen., A. A. G.

CHAPTER 2

Origin of the Tennessee Expedition of 1862

Our Army of the Tennessee have indulged in severe criticism at the slow approach of that army, which knew the danger that threatened us from the concentrated armies of Johnson, Beauregard, and Bragg, that lay at Corinth, (*sixteen miles off. W. P. G.*) (Sherman to U. S. S. Magazine, 1865.)

I hardly think we will want your troops. I do not think we will have an engagement short of Corinth. (*sixteen miles away. W. P. G.*) (General Grant to General Ammen, April 5, 1862, at noon on his arrival at the river, half an hour by steamer from Shiloh.)

In the last week of November, 1861, General Buell, who had been two weeks at Louisville, wrote to General-in-Chief McClellan, proposing an expedition up the Tennessee as high as Florence and Decatur, Alabama, which McClellan approved. On the 3rd January following he proposed to General Halleck the same expedition, to destroy the bridges over the Tennessee, as high up as Florence and Decatur, so as to sever the communication of the enemy between the north and south sides. This also would, by the occupation of Florence in force, have prevented all communication between Decatur and Memphis past Corinth, and past Humboldt, to New Madrid and Columbus, Kentucky, where the enemy were in force.

The occupation of both Florence and Decatur in force would have compelled the evacuation of Fort Donelson and Nashville without a fight, as afterwards Sherman's march from Savannah, Georgia, to the North, compelled the evacuation of Charleston, South Carolina. General Buell had proposed that the gunboats should run past Fort Henry, as afterwards, on Halleck's urgency, was done by Grant at Vicksburg; after starting down, as an experiment, in February 1863, two gunboats separately, which safely ran the batteries, but were of course captured below.

Buell's plan could have been accomplished, and would so have been by any commander less overcautious than Halleck, who could never be driven into an initiative movement likely to provoke a battle.[1] Halleck at that time expected and intended nothing, other than to capture Forts Henry and Donelson, and took care that Buell should have no immediate share in the honour of these captures, or any operations up the Tennessee; which will be plain before this narrative is concluded, (by necessary limitation,) and was upheld by the Washington ring. Before going into the subsequent correspondence, it may here be premised that Halleck, having seen the growing discontent with McClellan, during the winter of 1861-'62, had, as subsequent events prove, determined, if possible, to obtain McClellan's position as commander-in-chief.

The first commander, East or West, who should achieve any important success would of course be most likely to obtain the position; and when Mr. Lincoln, in January, 1862, exercised, ex officio, the duties of commander-in-chief, it was plain, as it was from the first of the war, that the Tennessee and Cumberland rivers offered the direct path to the most active and important operations of the war in the West. There was no one so likely to obstruct by his success the calculations of Halleck as General Buell. If he could be made use of in achieving any important object, without himself being an immediate actor, Halleck's point would be gained, as it eventually was by a course of intrigue, of which Buell, to his honour be it said, was morally

---

1. And had not the policy of the junto at Washington been in the way.

and intellectually indisposed, if not incapable, for any intrigue, for any purpose; while intrigue for every purpose was Halleck's characteristic practice and delight; and in this he, as will be seen, had resemblers, or perhaps followers or imitators, of various gradations.

In all the correspondence so far published, the name of General C. F. Smith, as a principal, does not appear; though we are told he was in command of the troops up the Tennessee from early in March to the 17th, and even a later date of that month. This means distinctly that he was either considered unfit for duty, or his name was used as a cover for ulterior purposes: the main purpose being to make him accountable for the location of the Union army at Shiloh. The only mention of any correspondence with C. F. Smith is a letter of Grant's, March 9th, to Smith, stating this: "General Halleck telegraphs me that when reinforcements arrive I may take the general direction."

On the 11th, Smith reached Savannah, Tennessee, whence he replied: "I wrote you yesterday to say how glad I was to find from your letter of the 11th of March you were to resume your old command, &c. C. F. Smith."

Reference, for the better understanding of the above statements, may now be had to the correspondence as to the Tennessee expedition, in which it will be seen that Halleck evades his concurrence in, and seeming origination of, the occupation of Florence, Alabama, in letters of March 4th, 6th, and 10th, 1862, which was the most obvious and immediate object, after the capture of Fort Henry, (in a military point of view,) as a means of closing the war. This was the last thing wanted then, at Washington, with whose ring Generals Halleck and Sherman were in close communion. And, as will be seen, to avoid Buell's urgency for the capture of Florence, he was placed under Halleck's command by the order of March 11, 1862. This was done, as must be repeated, that, by permitting A. S. Johnson's junction at Corinth, the expected battle would be out of Buell's district. After the capture of Corinth all operations were suspended on the Mississippi, to prolong the war and ruin Buell, who was too upright a man for the purposes of the ring.

> Johnson will not stand at Murfreesboro'; in fact, is preparing to get out of the way. Their plan seems to be to get in rear of the Tennessee, and in position to concentrate on Halleck or me. (Buell to McClellan, March 1, 1862.)

> I have telegraphed Halleck that it is important to seize Decatur, and thus cut General A. S. Johnson from Memphis and Columbus, &c., *(which Halleck would not do. W. P. G.)* (McClellan to Buell, March, 1862.)

As Halleck had in January been perfectly silent to Buell as to a visit of General Grant to St. Louis, to propose the Fort Henry affair, so he is, as will be seen, entirely silent as to any dispatch from McClellan urging the obvious capture of Decatur, which would first have required the occupation of Florence. This would have driven A. S. Johnson down into Alabama or towards Chattanooga, which was the last thing to be done for the accomplishment of Halleck and Sherman's objects which was to allow the junction of Johnson to the rebel force at Corinth. This junction would carry the war out of Buell's district and into that of Grant, held by him under Halleck's command, which was done. Halleck had undoubtedly grown jealous even of Grant at one time, or he pretended to be, in consequence of Donelson.

He wrote him no word of congratulation; imputed the capture mainly to C. F. Smith, *(it was right;)* and got up a row with Grant about going without leave to Nashville in February, 1862. (This was, of course, all understood,) or it was doubtless quieted by Sherman's agency when he reached Fort Henry on the 7th of March, 1862. He and Halleck had soon become aware that Grant was not a substantive man, and had sense enough to know it; which is a very great and his only merit, and effective as great it has been. It is the merit of the obstinate, but really docile mule, which, feeling its generic inferiority, will follow any thing of any sex in the shape of a horse however halt or blind, lame or spavined, the horse may be.

Nashville, March 1, 1862.

Johnson is evidently preparing to go towards the Tennessee. Decatur and Chattanooga seem to be the points of rendezvous at present. As soon as I can see my way a little, I will propose that we meet somewhere to consult, if agreeable to you." (*Which it was not, to Halleck.*) (General Buell to General Halleck.)

St. Louis, March 3, 1862.

I will make an appointment to meet you as soon as the Columbus movement is ended." (*Which he did not intend to do. W. P. G.*) (General Halleck to General Buell.)

On the same day General Buell informs General Halleck that "Johnson is moving towards Decatur, Alabama, and burning all the bridges as he goes," and asks, "What can I do to aid your operations against Columbus?"

On the 4th General Halleck writes Buell:

Why not come to the Tennessee, and operate with me to cut Johnson's line with Memphis and New Madrid?[2] Grant, with all available force[3] has gone up the Tennessee to destroy connection at Corinth, Jackson, and Humboldt, (*not the fact.*) Estimated strength of the enemy at New Madrid, Randolph, and Memphis is 50,000. It is a vital importance to separate them from Johnson's army: come over to Savannah or Florence, and we can do it. We then can operate either on Decatur or Memphis, or both, as may seem best, (*of which he had no intention not wishing to make Buell prominent, under the then circumstances.*)

On the 5th of March Buell answers:

Your views accord with my own generally, but some slight modification seems necessary. Can we not meet at Louisville in a day or so? I think it very important. The thing

---

2. Not the intention.
3. Not the fact.

which I think of vital importance is, that you seize and hold the bridge at Florence in force. Johnson is now at Shelbyville, some fifty miles south of this. I hope you will arrange for our meeting at Louisville. D. C. Buell. (General Buell to General Halleck)

Halleck answers March 6:

I cannot possibly leave here at the present time, (*of course not, W. P. G.*) Events are passing on so rapidly, that I must all the time be in telegraphic communication with Curtis, Grant, &c. We must consult by telegraph. News down the Tennessee that Beauregard has 20,000 men at Corinth, &c. Smith will probably be not strong enough to attack it. It is a great misfortune to lose that point, (*why lose it then?*) I shall reinforce Smith as rapidly as possible. If you could send a division round into the Tennessee, it would require only a small amount of transportation to do it. [Signed.]

H. W. Halleck.

Here now is as plain an intention of avoiding Buell as Grant put in practice a month later at Savannah. He says we must bear the great misfortune of losing Corinth, because there are 20,000 of the enemy there, we having 60,000 men or more; while all idea of Florence, from which, he says in his letter of the 4th, two days before, we could operate on Decatur and Memphis, is forgotten: and be it understood that Florence was the only attainable point from which we could so operate with any chance of success. That's why Halleck avoided Florence.

If there were 20,000 of the enemy at Corinth, these were 20,000 reasons why Johnson should not be allowed to join them with 20,000 more of the enemy. Even the unsuspicious Buell seems to have felt that here was the cold shoulder to his great yet obvious project, indorsed by McClellan the project of preventing the junction of the defeated Kentucky troops, under General Johnson, with troops from the Chesapeake and the Gulf, at Corinth, which project Halleck thus defeated. It seems that after the 6th of March there was a dispatch from Halleck of the same tenor on the 8th, to which Buell replies on the 9th, from Nashville, as follows:

I did not get your dispatch of the 6th until yesterday, (*suspicious*;) that of the 8th today. I suggest as follows: The enemy can move from one side of the river to the other at pleasure, (by the Florence bridge,) and if we attempt to operate on both sides, without equal means of transit, we are beaten in detail. Florence is the only point from which we can act centrally. If you occupy that point, I will reinforce you by water or join you by land. If we could meet, I think we could better understand each other. (*This Halleck persistently avoided purposely.*)   D. C. Buell.

Halleck answers, at St. Louis, March 10, 1862:

My forces are moving up the Tennessee river, &c. Florence was the point originally designated, but, on account of the enemy's forces at Corinth and Humboldt, it is deemed best to land at Savannah and establish a depot, (*which was never done the depot.*) The selection is left to C. F Smith, who commands the advance.

H. W. Halleck.

It is likely the dispatch of the 8th, which seems omitted above, had proposed a location on the west side of the river, as Buell intimates that till Florence is occupied, the enemy may move freely from side to side of the Tennessee by the bridge, and therefore insists on the occupation before joining Halleck by land or water, (and was right.) Here he (Halleck) states that Florence was the point originally designated, but on account of the enemy's forces at Corinth and Humboldt, he abandons a position, in the loss of which hundreds of millions and myriads of lives were involved and lost, which became the more essential from this occupation of Corinth, to say nothing of Humboldt, one hundred and twenty miles or more oft' from Florence, and from which no attack need to have been apprehended. No depot, properly speaking, was ever established at Savannah, except upon boats.

Halleck says, however, the selection between Florence and Savannah, on the east side of the river, was left to C. F. Smith. So now, if Sherman and Badeau and Grant and Bowman are credible witnesses, C. F. Smith disobeyed orders or directions here stated by Halleck, in choosing Pittsburgh on the west, instead of Florence or Savannah on the east, bank of the river. But this brave but infirm old soldier was indisposed or unfitted for any arduous intellectual duty after the capture of Fort Donelson, as was generally understood, and was hurt by an accident at Fort Henry, which, with other apparent causes, ended in his death the day of April, 1862. This fixes with certainty upon Sherman, Halleck, and Grant equal responsibility for their battlefield. But to return to the last letter of Buell, which could not have been of any avail, dated Nashville, March 10, 1862.

"The possession and absolute security of the country north of the Tennessee river," says Buell, "is of vital importance, both in a political and military point of view, and under no circumstances should it be jeopardized. It enables us, with the Tennessee as a base, to operate east, west, and south." (*This, of course, looked to the occupation of Florence, at the head of river navigation.*) Had the enemy occupied and fortified Florence, the conditions stated by Buell could not have existed before its capture. (*W. P. G.*) "With this view," he continues, "the establishment of your force on the east side of the river as high up as possible (Florence) is evidently judicious, and with the same view it would be unadvisable to change the line on which I propose to advance." (The line to Florence.) "I believe you cannot be too promptly or too strongly established on the Tennessee," (at Florence.) (Signed) " D. C. Buell."

Meantime, after Mr. Lincoln had issued his military orders, no doubt on the advice of Halleck and others most concerned against McClellan, such a change was made in Halleck's command, March 11th, as made further remonstrance on Buell's part unmilitary and unavailable, and thus, it is repeated, was organized on a wrong base, with a selfish and political purpose, the "Shiloh campaign," of which this is intended to be a treatise a campaign by which was clearly planned and inaugurated the battle resulting in the slaughter and defeat of Shiloh, which sent Halleck to Washington as commander-in-chief; and without any merit but a criminal defeat, wilfully induced, placed Grant and Sherman where they are; lengthened the war by at least a year, as was. the object; cost $800,000,000 and the lives and blood of many myriads of Union soldiers, with a pension list of at least $10,000,000 a year.

Two days before this last letter or message of Halleck's, March 8th, General Curtis gained the battle of Pea Ridge, and Hal leek, if he had chosen, had then 80,000 men for the capture and occupation of Florence, for which not 30,000 were requisite; but this capture, it is repeated, would have given Buell and Mitchell the honour of Johnson's defeat or retreat at, or from Decatur, and might have made Buell commander-in-chief at Washington, instead of Halleck, unless, as is probable, that had been arranged in Washington in November, 1861. It must here be understood, that the line of march for Buell from Nashville to Florence or Decatur, Alabama, was shorter and better than that to Savannah, had it been commenced the 5th or 10th of March, as it was not till the 20th that Johnson passed the danger, as he supposed it, of joining the Confederates at Corinth.

In a letter of March 18th, 1862, he (Johnson) says to Jeff. Davis:

> After Buell's capture of Nashville I marched southward and crossed the Tennessee at this point, (Decatur,) so as to co-operate or unite with General Beauregard at Corinth for the defence of the valley of the Mississippi. The passage is almost completed, and the head of my column is already with General Bragg at Corinth. The movement was deemed too hazardously the most experienced members of my staff, but the object warranted the risk. The difficulty of effecting a junction is not wholly overcome, but it approaches completion. Day after tomorrow, the 20th,

unless the enemy intercepts me, my force will be with Bragg.

As to the fall of Fort Donelson, General Johnson says:

I observed silence, as it seemed the best way to serve the cause and the country, (the South.) Exactly the reasons which prevented an investigation into the criminality of Shiloh. It would have checked or stopped volunteering, and might have changed the political complexion of Congress.

"The test of merit with the people is success," says Johnson. "It is a hard rule, but I think if, right. If I join this corps to the forces of General Beauregard, (I confess a hazardous experiment,) then those who are now declaiming against me will be without an argument."

And thus, through Halleck's ambition to be commander-in-chief, and perhaps stronger desire to avoid a battlefield, was the way paved to the battle of Shiloh, which cost Johnson his life, the Union 13,000 soldiers, and made that field of disgrace and slaughter the path to power and promotion, by those who were their ministers, (through the ring at Washington.)

Halleck had thus manoeuvred away forty days after the battle of Fort Henry before Buell's order, of March 18th, to McCook, to move from Columbia to Savannah. On the 20th of March, eight days after Badeau says Grant was restored to command, Halleck dispatches to Buell, as though General Smith were still in command at Savannah, though General Grant got there on the 17th. On the 22nd March, Buell states that he has a communication from General Grant at Savannah, of the 19th, which contains no intelligence of importance. He closes by asking if the bridge at Florence is destroyed, but is never answered. Its destruction was harmless to the enemy, as we were on the west bank of the river, preparing for the defeat at Shiloh. On the same day, March 22nd, he writes to General Grant, in answer to Grant's letter of the 19th; states that he has directed his advance at Columbia to open communications with General Grant at Savannah, and also asks if the bridge at Florence is destroyed, to which, no answer.

The above abstract of correspondence, to be returned to perhaps hereafter, will show: that Halleck, against the urgent advice of Buell, is responsible for the junction of Johnson and Beauregard at Corinth, and he and Grant are responsible for Buell's detention at Columbia. A single word that he was wanted, and, in less than two days, or one day, Buell could have crossed Duck river by flying bridges, and, if wanted, could have been at Savannah when Grant reached there, on the 17th of March, or sooner, but for Halleck; but there would have been no battle of Shiloh with its fatal results to all but these conspirators.

And now, having got the Army of the Tennessee near its camp at Shiloh, and shown how a month had been wasted for a selfish purpose in not having it at Florence a month before, let it be shown who was responsible for its location at Shiloh. The means by which the floods were assisted in keeping Buell back will be developed, and here, so far as private information is concerned, General Grant must bear the brunt of the delay and its consequences, meritorious or otherwise.

To do this satisfactorily, reference must be had to Badeau's *History of General Grant*, indorsed by General Grant himself, and one digression after another, and frequent repetitions, must be the tedious consequence. The third, or Shiloh chapter, of this *History of Badeau,* is made part of this commentary,[4] so that the reader, if not satisfied with the construction put upon the history by the commentator, can put upon the history a construction of his own, and no charge of garbling can be made, when so easily detected, by referring to Badeau.

Reference must, in considering this history, be made to the letters and reports of Generals Grant and Sherman, the life of Sherman by Bowman, with Sherman's indorsement, and such other official and unofficial evidence as will explain a narrative by no means connected, but as regular a commentary as such

---

4. The writer is compelled to omit this chapter of Badeau.

a history as Badeau's will permit. No account of the battle of Shiloh can have much consistency as to the connection or succession of events. But there need be no such contradictions as to time, events, or distances, as occur in Badeau, and all other accounts. The intention to confuse and deceive the casual reader is evident, and the laboured endeavour to show that Grant did not try to evade Buell on the 5th of April, gives plain proof of this evasion.

This evasion or avoidance of General Buell by Grant, on the 5th, is entire proof of the charge that he sedulously invited an attack, while as sedulously endeavouring to prevent Buell's knowing the danger, or having any share in repelling the expected attack; all of which, however tedious the process, the true and impartial historian is in duty bound to expose, as intimately connected with the most important, and extraordinary, and sanguinary battle of the rebellion.

Note. In this order of March 11, 1862, is found the first direct evidence of the intention and endeavor of the party at Washington to prolong the war. The matter had doubtless been understood and arranged before Halleck left Washington. The capture of Forts Henry and Donelson doubtless created alarm among these political schemers, who were bartering the lives and blood of Union soldiers for another quadrennium of power.

The capture of Florence was to be avoided, and it was for fear that Buell might follow up Mitchell's movement, and himself march on Florence, under authority of Halleck's letter of March 4, that this order was issued, which put the matter beyond the reach of Buell or McClellan; clipping McClellan's authority, and bringing Buell at once to a sense of subordination which he could not but approve. After the capture of Florence, that of Chattanooga, and the whole of the valley up to Harper's Ferry, so carefully avoided, might not have keen easily prevented before the election of 1864.

And thus this order sealed and signed the death warrant of 100,000 or more Union soldiers, and created Government bonds of a thousand millions or over. Who was, and who still is, and should be held responsible, and who were the willing instruments of such a wilful waste of patriot blood and national treasure, whose punishment should no longer be delayed?

CHAPTER 3

Tennessee Campaign of 1862, up to Savannah

I wish no prominent place in this war, I have no heart for it. I am perpetually embarrassed by my former associations with the South. (Sherman at Paducah and Columbus, Ohio)

I suppose we had a full supply of hay coming from Paducah, but think we were rather short. (Colonel Stuart's evidence for Sherman.)

Some of Grant's regiments arrived at Shiloh without cartridges, and had withstood and repelled the first day's terrific onset of a superior enemy at 4 p. m. (Sherman's letter, January, 1865.)

Headquarters District of Cairo, March 5, 1862.
Captain Hammond, Adjutant General:
Hold all steamboats till morning; notify all armed brigades and regiments to embark for Tennessee tomorrow.

Sherman.

This dispatch was the initiation of that Army of the Tennessee which marched by Shiloh and Memphis to Vicksburg; thence by Memphis and Chattanooga to Atlanta; thence by Savannah, Georgia, and Richmond, to Washington, where, after a grand triumph, it was disbanded in the summer of 1865.

The above dispatch reached Colonel Hicks, 40th Illinois

volunteers, about 9 p. m. of the 5th, and he, as brigade commander, made it known through his assistant adjutant general, to his subordinates during the course of the following forenoon. One of those subordinates (the writer) received the order to march while distributing arms to his regiment, about 9 a. m. of the 5th, or perhaps later in the day. It was, of course, greeted by his troops, with exceeding joy and great applause. Proceeding immediately to headquarters at Paducah, all commanders of regiments considered within the scope of the order received the following in addition:

(Special Order No. 74)

Headquarters District of Cairo,

Paducah, March 6, 1862.

The following regiments will embark today for Savannah, Tennessee river, and there report to Major General Smith.

The commanding officers will see that their regiments have eighty rounds of ammunition and all the means of transportation on hand. Baggage must be reduced to the minimum, and the quartermaster, Captain Pearse, will obtain a house in which to deposit all baggage left behind. (*No house for the sick. W. P. G.*)

Ohio 46th, Colonel Worthington; Ohio 48th, Colonel Sullivan; Illinois 40th, Colonel Hicks; Ohio 53rd; Colonel Appler; Ohio 72nd, Colonel Buckland.

The quartermaster will at once provide the transportation necessary.

By order of Brigadier General W. T. Sherman.

F. H. Hammond, A. A. G.

With this order the different chiefs of regiments repaired to the transportation office for boats, and generally left during the 6th of March, 1862. It will he observed, that in this order to raw troops, ignorant of, and unaccustomed to, service in the field, nothing is said in regard to army or hospital stores of any kind, or to any disposition of the sick, of which there was necessarily a large number, who could and should have been provided for in the many empty dwellings then in Paducah, left by rebels.

"Fort Henry had been captured," says Colonel Bowman, General Sherman's autobiographer, by "General Grant, on the 6th February, 1862," without explaining that the capture had been made through the intervention of Commodore Foote's gunboat fleet, sometime before that General's arrival, which, in justice to the gunboat fleet, should have been explained as it is here.

About the time of this capture it seems that General W. T. Sherman was ordered to Paducah, to take charge of forwarding supplies and reinforcements from that point. Whatever the characteristic energy imputed by his biographer may have effected in regard to the troops at Fort Donelson, it is certain that near a month later there was neither proper forage, ammunition, nor hospital stores for the five regiments ordered up the Tennessee on the 6th of March, 1862. That there were no proper hospital stores, and neither hay, oats, nor straw even, for the draft animals, might be accounted for by the exhaustion of this material of war for the consumption of the three divisions of McClernand, C. F. Smith, and L. Wallace, then at or near Fort Henry, which divisions, however, reached Savannah in about the same state of destitution; and General Sherman, a month later, admits that some of the regiments reached camp Shiloh even without ammunition. But hospitals and quarters for the sick were plenty at Paducah. There was no possible excuse for the extravagance, impolicy, and inhumanity of hauling sick men to crowded boats, where to properly care for them was impossible; and to carry them with the army, as was done, to die, was simply barbarous.

The surgeons, of their own motion, found empty houses, and did the best they could for the dangerously sick, though all weak and ailing men should, as a matter of expediency if not humanity, have been left behind. The 6th was a raw, windy, snowy March day, worthy more of Labrador than Tennessee, near the line of which last we were. The mud was just sufficiently frozen for the horses to break through at every other step. This narrator, with his command, was near two miles from his boat, and, with unbroken mule teams, to reach the river during daylight, with his camp equipage and stores, was a very uneasy job.

Of the above-named regimental commanders ordered up the Tennessee, Colonel Worthington, 46th Ohio, was the only educated military officer. He was sufficiently provident to take on board ten days' additional stores of army rations for his men and provender (nothing but shelled corn) for his mules and horses. Of the eighty rounds of ammunition ordered, but thirty could be had, and that at 11 p. m., or after.

His stores were all on board, and he embarked (just one month before the battles of the 6th and 7th of April following,) at 3 a. m. of the 7th of March, 1862. The boat (Adams) neared Fort Henry, about noon next day, and about all the boats which had left Paducah the day before were still there, besides many others intended for the transportation of the three divisions from Fort Donelson to the future field of Shiloh.

Drawing up on the west side to make inquiries, the 40th Ohio found itself next the boat of the 5th Ohio cavalry, Colonel Taylor. On inquiry it was found that this regiment had been there near a week, waiting orders, and that there was one gunboat and perhaps a single transport gone up the river. During our two weeks' delay at Paducah, there had been rumours of ill treatment of Union men at Savannah, who had expected we would have immediately taken possession of Florence, Alabama, as urged by General Buell, immediately after the capture of Fort Henry. On this reliance many had expressed their sentiments too freely, and thereby suffered in various ways.

A general draft of all men fit to bear arms had been contemplated, and as it is one of the first rules of an intended invasion to move to the objective point as rapidly as possible, it was concluded, *nem. con.,* to proceed, as there was no signal for the boat from Fort Henry. Beyond this there was some chance of forage for the teams before the advance of the army, momentarily expected, and the regiment accordingly steamed on up. The colonel of the 46th would have continued all night, and urged the master of the boat to do so, but he was apprehensive, he said, of masked batteries upon either shore, and nothing was left but reluctant acquiescence. The colonel's diary of the 8th is as follows:

Saturday, March 8th, 1862.— A fair frosty morning. Started about sunrise, and about 8. 30 a.m. stopped at Britt's landing, and took aboard 98 bushels and 426 sheaves of oats. Stopped at Clifton and other landings, but heard nothing satisfactory. Got to Savannah about sunset. Found there one half of the 40th Illinois, Lieutenant Colonel Booth. Took command, and threw out 120 men as pickets also a patrol, which took up forty or fifty stragglers of the 40th, who were invading the houses, and, as the people thought, threatening mischief, there being a bar on board the boat. Saw a Union man, Mr. W. H. Cherry, and got him to send a servant to Waynesboro, thirty miles north-west, for information.

Heard that the rebel authorities, in anticipation of our arrival, were hauling stores from the river below, around by Florence, to Iuka, all of which would have been stopped but for the delay in sending troops to Florence a month before. This half of the 40th Illinois had passed Fort Henry in the night of the 6th, and, taking little note of circumstance or time, had reached Savannah about an hour by sun. It might have been in danger but for the arrival of the 46th, which last it was afterward rumoured, at home. had been captured by ignorantly going ahead of the fleet, &c. But the arrival was roost timely. From Mr. Cherry was derived information that the rebel authorities were active in the vicinity that there had been a draft *en masse* of the able-bodied male population the previous Thursday, and the drafted men were ordered to muster at Savannah on Monday, the 10th of March following.

Deeming it his duty to get as full a report as possible of the state of affairs in the vicinity for the information of General C. F. Smith on his arrival, he, as stated in the above diary extract, employed and dispatched a scout in the direction of Waynesboro. During the night many refugees came to the boat from the west side of the river. Many came into the town from the eastward on hearing of the arrival of Union troops, and perhaps more than a thousand drafted men from all quarters crowded the little village next day.

On Sunday, the 9th, the 46th had a dress parade, and, in connection with the incoming refugees from the rebel draft, this Sunday was pronounced the liveliest day the little town of less than one thousand inhabitants had ever witnessed. At about 2 p. m. several officers of the 46th went up in the gunboat Lexington, by invitation of Captain Quin, to Pittsburgh landing, eight miles above, and threw, perhaps, a dozen shell into the interior, to which there was no reply.

Savannah is the county seat of Hardin county, and is joined on the west by McNairy county. From the drafted refugees mainly of these two counties the 46th received during the day forty or fifty recruits. Night came on with no news of' the fleet below, much to the surprise of the 46th Ohio, which, being the last regiment to embark at Paducah had had little thought of being the first full regiment to to reach its destination in advance of the Army of the Tennessee, so famous afterwards in the war.

On Monday, the 10th, daylight came on with rain. Lieutenant Colonel Booth, of the 40th Illinois, found himself out of stores, and the colonel of the 46th, declining his request to forage upon the people of the town, gave him two days' rations, and an order to proceed down the river and look up the army fleet. This was deemed an affront which Colonel Hicks, of the 40th Illinois, and commander of the brigade, was disposed to resent, and did afterwards resent, as an insult, to himself and his regiment.

A river boat, crowded with troops, being the last place suitable for sick men, they were got out today, and put into a vacant house near the river, which had been emptied by its owner, who was an officer in the Confederate army. He had, however, with usual southern hospitality, authorized Mr. Cherry to allow its occupation by our sick or wounded, should our troops appear in his absence: doubtless, also, aware of the good policy of making a virtue of necessity.

Arrangements were also made for the fitting up of a new frame church, with the consent of the village authorities, for a government hospital; it having been understood that here was to be a large army depot for weeks or months, whence the troops would march to break up railroads, or rebel camps at Corinth, Jackson, and Humboldt, (humbug.) During Sunday and Monday the pickets of the 46th had captured half a dozen or more of rebel scouts and horsemen, with their horses and mules, and learned that there was a large force of Confederate troops gathering or expected about Florence, Tuscumbia, Eastport, and Iuka, then expecting our attack on the first-named place, as it had been expected a full month before.

Tuesday, the 11th, was a fair, cool morning. The troops were brought ashore to clean up the boat, and most of the sick were made more comfortable in the improvised hospitals, the villagers doing all service in their power; for which they had and still have the grateful recollections of the troops and their commander Mr. William H. Cherry being among the foremost in this friendly, and, indeed, charitable ministration, for which no provision had been made by our commander.

Several Confederates were captured today, and among them one of the regular rebel cavalry, who had been sent in to see what was going on among the Yankee invaders of the "sacred soil."

The steamer *Golden Gate* came up about noon, and announced the Union fleet of boats at hand. The 46th Ohio was paraded on the hill above the landing on open ground, where a fair view could be had of .the approaching Army of the Tennessee.

The first boats came in sight about 2 p. m., some two miles down the river, and it was a sight fraught with splendour for the 46th Ohio a spectacle beheld by no other regiment in the army. The weather was soft and fine, and one or more flags floated over every boat. Nearly every regiment had a band of music, and in this, till then, sequestered region, occurred a scene of martial activity and festivity, never before witnessed in the Union. Unexpected, grand, and indeed terrible, it was, to the inhabitants along the forest-girded banks of the Tennessee.

It was soon, however, discovered, that however beneficial to the people of the vicinity and to the interests of the Union had been the arrival of the 46th Ohio in advance of the army, it was anything but agreeable to General C. F. Smith and the general officers of the Army of the Tennessee. General Smith, irritable from ill-health and ill-habits, was furious at what he denominated the presumption and insubordination of a colonel of volunteers in preceding such an expedition in command of a regular officer of the army of the United States and major general of Union volunteers. He refused to receive the colonel's report, and rebuked him for disregard of military etiquette in not passing his report through his commander of brigade and division, with whom his orders had nothing to do; and to do this would have been impossible, without disobeying the order of the 6th, (No. 74,) which was peremptory to proceed to Savannah and there report to Major General C. F. Smith, who was on the leading boat of the fleet, where the colonel of the 46th found and offered him his report.

It also soon appeared that the division commander was equally irate at the too prompt arrival of the 46th, whose colonel he had snubbed at midnight for being slack in his departure, while he was getting on stores and hunting up ammunition, which the general of division not only failed to supply, but he refused to give an order for ammunition at Paducah, intended for a regiment without arms. But Colonel W. got it.

By his prompt arrival the colonel of the 46th had prevented the pressure into the rebel service of perhaps a thousand Union men, and had added hundreds to fill up the deficient Union regiments. Instead of approbation for the result of his prompt obedience to a peremptory order, his reward was the enmity of those above him, who had failed in their duty, and an attempt at his degradation for performing his own. (See note at the end of the chapter.)

Colonel Hicks, the brigade commander, was an old Illinois militia officer, a benevolent and brave man, but proud and obstinate, as he was ignorant of, and opposed to strict military discipline. Without much education of any kind, he was boastful that in the Mexican war he had acquired, and professed, great contempt for regular officers and army regulations. This contempt for all military law he had carried out to the fullest extent at Paducah, refusing to subject his troops (good men as they were and of excellent material for soldiers) to any discipline whatever.

He had in consequence been held in arrest by General Smith for weeks or even months at Paducah, and his men, instead of being sent to the field, had been retained in quarters, as utterly unskilled, in consequence of their colonel's practices and principles, and therefore unfitted for campaign duty.

Under this officer, at war as he professed to be with all regular officers and with strict discipline, was the colonel of the 46th Ohio brigaded by the general of division, with a purpose of his own, and anything but friendly to the older graduate. When visiting his pickets at Paducah, near those of Colonel Hicks, he had found it the practice of these vigilant watchers of the Illinois, to gather in squads, of two or three or more, around a fire, on or off the picket line, then and there to stack arms, by driving their bayonets into the "bloodless sheath" of the muddy soil, and pass the time at seven-up, poker, or some such absorbing game of cards, and all with their colonel's entire approbation sometimes perhaps a looker on himself.

On reporting this in a quiet way to the brigade commander, he told his subordinate a long story of his experience with the stiff and stately regulars, tyrannizing over the innocent recreations of their men, of whom they should have been like him, even as it were a father to his troops, as he was. As to amending the habits of the sentinels, "it was hard to teach an old dog new tricks." On representing the case to General Sherman he agreed with Colonel Hicks, and concluded to let matters proceed in the regularly irregular militia routine, or no routine at all.

So the West Point man had to give it up, &c., &c., forbidding his own men on pain of imminent death or disgrace, if ever in danger, from indulging on picket duty in such agreeable but dangerous and most unmilitary practices; and it was by such practices that many regiments were surprised, posts lost, and thousands of men killed and captured, in the early period of the war. But to return to the brigade commander at Savannah. He had on arrival landed on the west side of the river, thus dividing his brigade. On the morning of the 12th, the adjutant of the 46th reported this fact, and stated that, the yawl of the Adams being gone, he could not get his morning report over the river. He was told to send a copy of the report to the A. A. G. of the division, and get the report over as soon as he could get a boat. There was no forage to be had in the country for the teams, and the colonel of the 46th, having purchased a lot of corn in the husk, was busily getting it on board, supposing, of course, the expedition would not stop short of Florence, where feed for teams would be still more difficult of supply, and therefore he left the care of his report to the adjutant.

At 1 p. m. Colonel Hicks had the colonel of the 46th arrested for failing to send over his report. Stating the case to Sherman, he got a release at 5 p. m., with a letter from Hicks, in which he was assured the arrest had been fully approved by Sherman, who knew that no one but General C. F. Smith could legally make an arrest. This, however, exposed his animus toward Colonel Worthington of the 46th, who was reported at home as degraded for misconduct and neglect of duty, in preceding the army without orders. The object of brigading him under such an enemy of regular officers as Colonel Hicks had been attained, and soon after Hicks was displaced for the appointment of another brigade commander, also with a personal. object on the part of Sherman, as will appear in the course of this treatise; which, let it here be remembered, will not be cumbered with any more such personalities, if possible to be avoided.

We have now the Army of the Tennessee at Savannah, instead of Florence; the reason of stopping short of which place will be developed hereafter, so far as present information can lead to such development.

The division commander thus vented his rage at the early arrival of the 46th Ohio at Savannah, on those of its sick men his negligence or inhumanity had failed to provide for at Paducah, and this after having snubbed its commander for being late at that place, to repair his neglect in not giving orders to his colonels to take on additional stores for such an expedition and leave their sick behind.

Note:—

[EXTRACT FROM THE DIARY OF AN OFFICER OF THE
ARMY OF THE TENNESSEE.]

Savannah, Tennessee, Tuesday, March 12, 1872.

A lot of sick men were lodged for the day in a house near the river bank, owned by a Confederate officer named Martin, with leave of his brother to use it and his own leave, through Mr. Cherry. Martin's wife I had seen in the morning, who made no objection to the use of the house, which was destitute of any furniture, and did not tell me there was anything to be injured, as I understood there was not. Being in a room above stairs about sunset, I heard that she was complaining that mischief had been done. I went down and told the sick men to go to the boat. Going out, I found Mrs. Martin complaining to General Sherman, who asked me angrily what the men were doing in the house. I said they were sick men, put in the house by permission of its owner, while the boat was being cleaned out. He answered that it was an outrage to put men in a house where there were a parcel of women, and ordered some soldiers of a Missouri regiment to turn the men out. The sick were going as fast as their strength would permit. I clutched his arm and requested him to be quiet, as I had ordered the men out, and he saw that they were going out. He repeated his order to clear them out very violently, and in the most silly and brutal manner; but no one seemed disposed to obey an order to commit violence upon sick men, thus barbarously brought up from Paducah, instead of being sent home, both as a matter of humanity and economy.

Savannah, Tennessee, March 12, 1862.

The undersigned, citizens of Savannah, Tennessee, and vicinity, hereby declare, that the presence of the 46th Ohio volunteer regiment on the 3rd instant, proved most opportune in preventing the arresting and pressing into service of persons subject to the draft or detail ordered by the State authorities. Refuge was thereby afforded to those who had to leave home on account of the draft, and in preventing many of them from being pressed into the rebel army, and adding a considerable number of recruits to the Union army. The troops under Colonel Worthington have been quiet and orderly, committing no trespass or intrusion on our citizens or their property. That they were actively engaged as scouts and pickets is proven by their capture of a number of the rebel cavalry. Information of hostile operations was sedulously sought for, and active measures taken for their suppression by the officers in command. And we further declare, that the opportune arrival of said regiment here gave great satisfaction to our community, and by their efficiency and good conduct they merit our thanks and approval, as they will doubtless receive that of the national Government and all true friends of the Union.

W. H. Cherry, H. Stephens, J. S. Berry, B. Hinkle, George L. Morrow, Donald Campbell, H. H. Brogles, I. N. Kindel, I. N. Herring, C. W. Morris, Bert S. Russell, B. B. Alexander, J. I. Trist, D. T. Street, T. N. Caldwell, T. G. Lee, R. T. Picket, John H. Maxwell, John Williams, E. Walker, W. N. Maxwell, Win. Russell, John W. Eccles, J. D. Donahue, C. C. Franks, Thos. Maxwell, J. S. Winton, W. W. Thurston, Robt. Meadar, W. D. Booth, T. L. Puckett, D. D. Crook, T. F. Frazier, R. H. Russell.

Chapter 4

Eastport Expedition

Sherman, on the 14th March, went to Tyler's landing, whence the 6th Ohio marched to Burnsville, on the Memphis and Charleston railroad, some miles east of Oorinth, which was destroyed, and returned unmolested to Savannah. (Hon. H. Greeley.)

On the 14th of March, Sherman, with the leading division of Grant's army, passed up the Tennessee on transports, and, after making a feint of landing at Eastport, dropped down the stream and disembarked at Pittsburgh landing, (all on the 14th.) (*Bowman & Irving's Sherman and his Campaigns.*)

General C. F. Smith pushed forward troops to Eastport, on the Tennessee, but ultimately took Pittsburgh landing as the initial point. (*E. D. Mansfield's Lives of Grant and Colfax.*).

C. F. Smith took command of the expedition, and while the captain of Donelson remained in disgrace at Fort Henry, the troops were pushed forward as far as Eastport, on the Tennessee. The operations, however, were without results, and Smith returned to Pittsburgh landing, on the western bank of the Tennessee. *(Badeau's History of Grant.)*

By the above the honour of this Eastport affair seems to remain easy as between the claims of Smith and Sherman to the same, while Grant is entirely accessory, and was, perhaps, more than so in reality, though Smith bears the blame. Now, there may be many inferences deduced from the above-cited quotations by the admirers of these two rebellion-risen commanders. Inseparable in the origin and cause of their success as the twin brothers of the old Dorian mythology, though which is the pugilist and which the cavalier their admirers may take their own time and way to determine. (*Both are of the ring.*)

From this category of admirers may, perhaps, be excluded that most benevolent and impracticable political philosopher and too practical utilitarian sage, Greeley, never satisfied without the evolution of results from causes. In such earnest and laudable research he has found it essential to tell, in order that actions may have results, that Sherman went to Tyler's Landing, whence the 6th Ohio (under the general's command, of course,) marched to Burnsville, some miles out of Corinth, which (Burnsville or Corinth?) was destroyed, and returned unmolested to Savannah. It is difficult to distinguish as to the merit of these wonderful performances, if accomplished; but it seems plain that the 6th Ohio should have the palm, not as to the imaginary destruction of Burnsville or Corinth, &c., but, being at the time (March 14th) at Nashville, Tennessee, its march must, if made, have far exceeded in celerity that of Nero, the consul, (not the fiddling firebrand,) from Venusia to the Metaurus.

There seems, at the same time, little or no disposition on the part of Sherman's admirer, Bowman, to impute that merit to his patron, which, according to Badeau and Sherman, properly belongs to C. F. Smith, the real hero of Fort Donelson, if there was one. The fast friend (*fidus Achates*) and uncertain eulogist of the President is clearly entitled to the merits, and still more clearly to the demerits, of this wonderful, dangerous, and mysterious expedition, comparable only to that of Jason, (or possibly Mason,) to Colchis after the Golden Fleece time out mind.

This expedition is, or was, as brilliant, according to Greeley, as it is terrible, according to Draper. If we are to believe this most erudite, critical, and most veracious historian, Sherman lost many men and horses in the swollen streams, striving to reach the Memphis and Charleston railroad. If any men and horses were really lost, their record has been kept more quiet than that of the three horses which were not killed under Sherman at Shiloh, unless, like the knight of old, he killed them to prevent their captivity by the enemy.

The venerable Mansfield makes the Eastport honour uncertain, but drops the matter as provocative of inquiry by curious readers.

The true history of this affair, so studiously covered up by Badeau and Bowman, is taken from the diary of an officer who was an actor in this worse than useless expedition, which was most fortunately arrested, as it might plainly have produced the most ruinous results to the troops engaged in it though with that cost if Sherman, its instigator, could thereby have been set aside for a more worthy commander at Shiloh.

Savannah, Tennessee, March 14, 1862.
About 1 p. m. Sherman's troops left on an expedition to Mississippi, and tied up a few miles below Eastport. Rain last night and rain all day after 12 m. We were to have left for the interior at midnight, but about 11 p. m. had orders that the start was postponed till 2 a. m. (15th,) the river rising six or eight inches an hour, and filling a bayou or thoroughfare next the hill, which will be impassable long before noon to morrow.

Saturday, *March 15,* 1862. Up at half past 12; raining, as it had been all night. The expedition had been ordered, with two days' cooked provisions, to march out and break up the Memphis and Charleston railroad and return. A useless job, unless we can effect a lodgement, which does not seem intended. Started in the rain about 3 a. m., though from the rising water it was plain we would soon have to return. Went out about three or four miles, over a road impracticable for artillery without repair, and were there stopped by a creek backed up from the river and several feet deep upon the road. My regiment, having charge of the artillery, I went back and reported to Sherman, who ordered a return about 7 or 8 a. m. At the bayou found the 54th Ohio *zouaves*, Colonel Smith, wading back breast deep.

A very silly expedition under the circumstances, and adding hundreds of weakly men to the sick list.

The high water was fortunate, as had we got a few miles farther toward the railroad, the division would have been captured, as the rebels were in force about Iuka, and A. S. Johnson was just passing his troops over the route from Decatur to Corinth, expecting the occupation of Florence every hour of every day after the capture of Fort Henry, up to the time he concentrated with Bragg and Beauregard, about the 20th of March, 1862. (W. P. G.)

This Eastport affair demands attention, on account of the endeavor, by imputing it to Smith or dropping it entirely, to conceal a characteristic blunder of Sherman's in the opening of the campaign, which was repeated by him whenever an opportunity offered throughout the war. It was the blunders, and nothing else but blunders and far worse, at Shiloh, which have given him his present position, and blunders alone characterized him in the advance on Savannah, Tennessee, as improvident, reckless, violent, and unjust, while his advance on Savannah, Georgia, earns for him the reputation of the "Attila of the age." It took all day of the 15th to get the troops and artillery on board the fleet. Left soon after midnight, and on the morning of Sunday, the 16th, the boats tied up at Pittsburgh, which also deserves attention, as this first landing of troops at Pittsburgh is imputed by Grant to C. F. Smith.

Note. This most extraordinary and indeed insane movement could not be accounted for by the writer till he found ample evidence that it was intended to cover Halleck's avoidance of the occupation of Florence for personal purposes. It would not have been undertaken had there been any probability of its success. Time will doubtless develop that these operations of Hal-

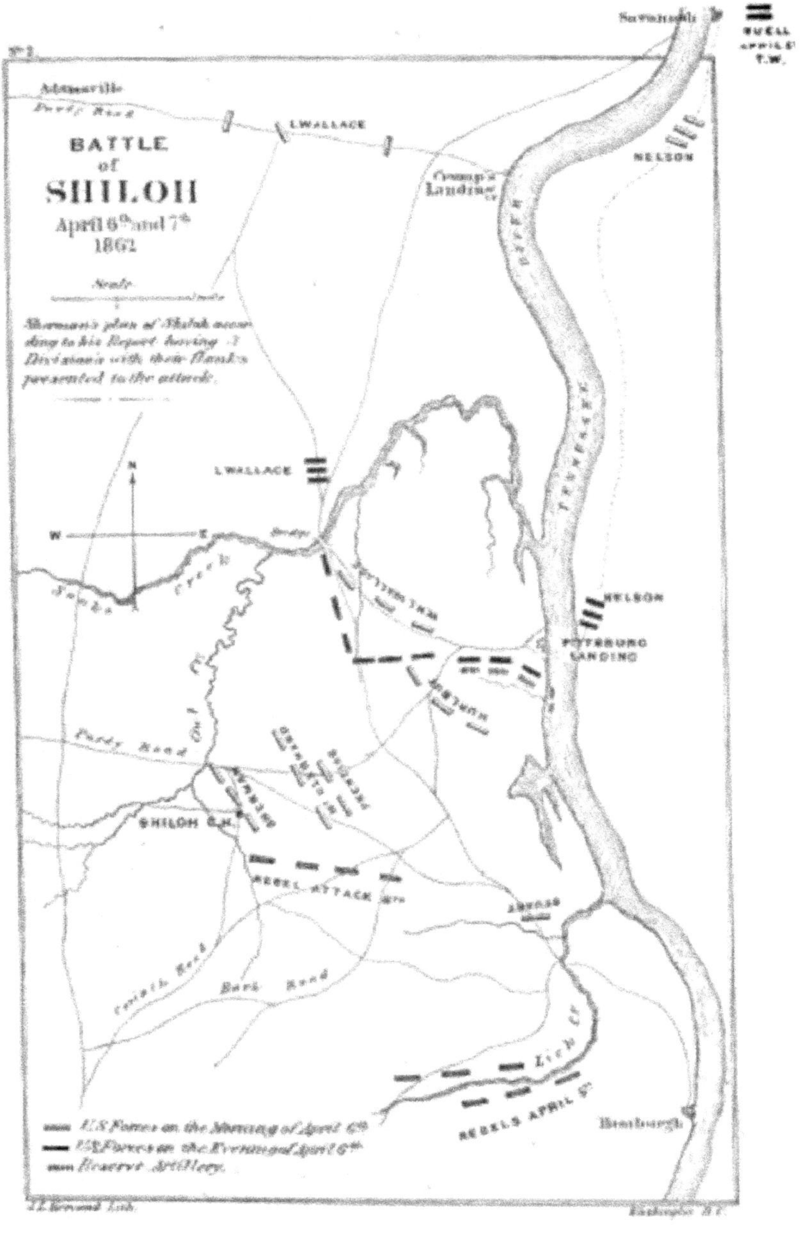
BATTLE
of
SHILOH
April 6th and 7th
1862
L.WALLACE
NELSON
L.WALLACE
N
W
E
Snake Creek
PITTSBURG
LANDING
NELSON
Purdy Road
SHILOH C.H.
REBEL ATTACK
Bark Road
Lick Cr
REBELS APRIL 5th

leck's had their origin in Washington, having several purposes one to supplant McClellan, one to prolong the war, and beyond this to put Halleck, Grant, and Sherman into the positions they attained, at the sacrifice of hundreds of millions and myriads of lives.

CHAPTER 5

Into Camp Shiloh

A small stream that rises in the field in front flows to the north along my whole front. (*This faces the division to the west, W. P. G.*) I saw that the enemy designed to pass my left flank, and fall upon Generals McClernand and Prentiss, whose line of camps was almost parallel with the Tennessee river, and about two miles back from it. (*Sherman's Report of Shiloh.*) (The Tennessee running due north at Shiloh.)

These divisions are also faced east or west, and are in a line parallel with Sherman's division, exposing their flanks to the attack from the South, (see map 2) which was about an equivalent arrangement to that which existed. (*W. P. G.*)

Sherman's 5th division went into camp three miles out from Pittsburgh landing, on the 18th and 19th of March, and Hurlbut's division, (the 4th,) from half a mile to a mile out about the same time, and to the right and left of the Corinth road, with little or no order whatever. C. F. Smith's and McClernand's divisions came out from the 20th to the 22nd of March. Smith's, the 2nd division, was scattered along the upper Purdy road from half a mile to a mile or over, out west from Pittsburgh landing.

McClernand's (1st) division was encamped in better order and on better ground than any other. His left was & little east of the main Corinth road, about four hundred yards nearly due north from Sherman's centre at Shiloh church, and bending a little back or eastward from the centre to the right or north; the ground was, in general, wooded on the east of this camp, with open ground on the west, which was a good arrangement for defence, so far as it went.

Its general direction made an angle of about seventy degrees toward the north-west, with the direction of Sherman's line at its centre. Sherman's statement of his centre as being at Shiloh church is about the only correct statement in that report, except, perhaps, his account of his wanton destruction of a battery of his own artillery, and his desertion of what organized troops he had left at the most dangerous hour of the day, 10 o'clock m., as he specifies, but only one brigade, not two, as he says.

Badeau's map of Shiloh, corrected both by Grant and Sherman, has his (Sherman's) centre far east of the Corinth road; while the official map, corrected by the same authorities, puts the same centre five hundred yards or more west of the Corinth road, so that both maps contradict the division report and each other. Badeau's map refuses, or throws back the right or 1st brigade of Sherman's, which was the reverse of the fact. This map also throws the 1st brigade across the Purdy road, where it was not, but where one of its regiments should have been.

The two extreme right regiments of the army lay directly along the lower Purdy road, which passed between the field and staff quarters on one side and the company quarters on the other. Sherman's division was on a line concave, instead of convex to the front.

It is most probably arranged convex on the map to produce the impression that Sherman's centre, behind which he had his headquarters, was the most advanced part of the line, as it was, south-west towards Corinth, but not southward.

The camp of General B. M. Prentiss, established ten or twelve days before the battle under General Grant's immediate direction, was located with its right over a mile from the left of Sherman. Its centre was in latitude near a quarter of a mile south of Shiloh church, or a little south of east from Sherman's centre. It had seven regiments scattered without order along a distance of half it's proper front, which would have been over three-quarters of a mile.

On Badeau's map a third brigade, which is a fiction, is thrown in to fill up the vacancy. The left of Prentiss was in nearly a north and south line with the right of Stuart's (2nd) brigade of Sherman's (5th) division, and was about eighty rods south of Stuart, whose three regiments were dumped down anywhere, near a mile from the Hamburgh Ford of Lick Creek, half a mile from its mouth at the river. It has been asserted, according to Whitelaw, Reed, and others, as an excuse for so exposing and detaching this brigade, that as Buell's troops were to be posted at Hamburgh, two miles above on the river, the exposure would cease when this posting should occur.

Now, Buell's advance division reached Savannah, eight miles below Pittsburgh, before noon of the 5th. The same afternoon the rebel army was concentrated westward, at and from the south-east bend of Lick Creek. This bend is about a mile north-west of Hamburgh, on the river, and the same distance nearly due south of Stuart and Prentiss, making the right of the enemy a little over a mile from the river at Hamburgh, according to Badeau's map. So that, if the intention of posting Buell at Hamburgh had been carried out, the rebel army might have been attacked at 4 p. m. (5th) or after, on its right and rear, by Buell, and on its front by our army of 40,000 men, at Shiloh. Its capture and dispersion would have been inevitable. But, if done, this would have been done by Buell's troops, and was not in accordance with the views of Grant, Sherman, and Halleck, in the field, nor the Committee on the Conduct of the War, &c.,.at Washington. This digression will be repeated whenever opportunity offers, to show how and why the Union troops at Shiloh were slaughtered for personal purposes, after their betrayal into security, for purely or impurely political objects, by direction of those in power.[1]

---

1. The war was cultivated as old hunters cultivate she-wolves, for wolf-scalps for the sum of so much a head or scalp.

After which digression return is made to the camp. Grant and Sherman, to make the front look respectable, have posted the right of Prentiss half a mile nearer Shiloh than it was, while the brigade of Stuart, the only body of troops placed anywhere near right on the front, is separated from the left of Prentiss by a gap of half a mile, which did not exist, so as to close the gap towards Shiloh. To cover this fictitious gap there is very cunningly placed a body of troops which was not there till after the battle.

The very worst fictional feature of this map of Grant's and Sherman's is the poking in of McClernand's left flank between Sherman and Prentiss, over half a mile east from its true position. This is an attempt to close upon paper a gap of over a mile, which did really exist in fact, and which Sherman swears did not exist at all, and did exist; for Buell's troops, which were to be sent to Hamburgh, as they would have been sent, were it not necessary, as he says, to have had a "Shiloh" trial of pluck, So they were left at Savannah, were Buell's troops. This gap was a bait; the bait took, and took with it 13,000 Union soldiers on the 6th and 7th of April, 1862.

This gap was not only the key-point, but the wide, open highway to the flanks and rear of the Union line; and this is the key Grant says Sherman held into the inside of the line, if line that can be called, without military connection; without connecting roads, front, flank, or rear; without proper guards; without defences, for fear they would invite an attack; without anything especial but the gaps, like the intervals between herds of buffaloes scattered over the western plains, if buffaloes do scatter at all, even when out of danger. The least broken ground on this battlefield of about ten square miles, except that of McClernand's 1st division, was the line of this front, of about two and a half to three miles from Stuart's left to the extreme right of Sherman's 1st brigade.

This extreme right rested on a height one hundred and twenty rods north of Owl Creek. There was a rivulet, with swampy borders, between the left regiment, the 53rd Ohio, which separated it about two hundred yards from the 57th, on its right. Over this swamp there was no causeway or connection with the centre, but by the high land in the rear. The ground on this line being unbroken by ravines, was easily defensible from infantry, and no line ever more required defences than did this line of Sherman's three right brigades, and defences sufficient could have been made by all the troops in an hour. Located on the upland, bordering a creek fifty to one hundred and fifty yards in front, with a wooded, bushy border, the line was approachable and was approached within half-musket shot by an an enemy remaining almost entirely unseen.

Beyond the creek four hundred to six hundred yards in front, was a range of low hills, commanding the camp, and forty to sixty feet or more above its level, which level was thirty to forty feet above the creek bottom immediately in front. The left might have been so located as to be completely protected by the Tennessee river, but it was so posted as to be turned easily, as it was turned soon after the attack on the 6th. On the extreme right, Owl Creek might have been used to strengthen that flank, but it was left as a mask for a hostile approach. Had this right flank been attacked, as was Sidney Johnson's intent, by even a single brigade, at the same time with the left, and held its ground no better than the 53rd Ohio, under Sherman's immediate direction, the destruction of the Union army before noon would have been inevitable.

The same result would have occurred at or about noon, had our right been turned by the rebel flanking force, which for several hours was repelled by the 1st brigade of the 5th division, which brigade was detached under the charge of Sherman's aides, and, deserted by them and him, was left unsupported and alone, far on the extreme right and front of the Union line of battle. (See Sherman's report.)

Such as is above imperfectly described, was the battlefield of Shiloh, selected by Sherman with demoniac sagacity and approved by Grant, before the troops went into camp on the 18th and subsequent days of March, 1862 chosen with as much anxious and personally interested sagacity as marked the patriotic purpose of the great German liberator Arminius (Hermann) in choosing among the forests of the Lippe (Detmold now) that battlefield for the destruction of Varus and his legions, denominated, as one part of it is, the *mord kessel* (death pot) to the present day.

To fix the day of our being ordered into camp the following diary extracts may be of interest:

> Pittsburg Landing, March 18, 1862.
> Went to Sherman's boat, the Continental, for orders, and was told to get everything off the boat of the 46th Ohio at once, and to the camp about three miles out near Shiloh church. During the night the 3rd Iowa and 81st Ohio had completely clogged the road, which they did not clear for the teams of the 46th till near 2 p. m. By night the teams were worn out and had to stop. There seems no order or regularity about anything. Every volunteer regiment is allowed to dump its camp down anywhere and in everybody's way.

> Wednesday, March 19th, 1862.
> A damp morning, after rain during the night. At 8.30 a. m. saw Sherman on the Hannibal, and reported that the road was clogged by the regiment and would soon be impassable. Without waiting for my suggestion that the road should be left open or I could not get out, he said very brusquely that be could not act on my mere *ipse dixit*; that his engineer had examined and reported on the road, (he had no engineer.) I then suggested that one thousand men on the road towards the proposed camp could put it in passable order in a few hours, and requested that I might be myself permitted to repair the road. He said he would do nothing with it today, but might tomorrow, (nothing, however, was done.) Rode out to the camp about noon, stepped off the ground for the ten companies, and had my own tent pitched about sunset.

CHAPTER 6

How Buell was hurried up

I believe you are as brave, patriotic, and just as the great prototype, Washington; as unselfish, kind-hearted, and honest as a man should be. (Sherman to Grant on his appointment as Lieutenant General.)

But this much is certain: The rebels were repelled in their last attack on Sunday without any assistance from Buell that turned the scale. (*Grant in Badeau. See Grant's report. W. P. G.*)

The first thing that will call the attention of the critical reader in the autobiographies of Grant and Sherman by Badeau and Bowman, is the fact that General Buell is charged with tardiness, while the Army of the Tennessee is in danger of attack and need of assistance. Grant says, in *Badeau*, page 67, that on the 17th March he removed his headquarters to Savannah. "The attention of the rebels in this part of the country had now become concentrated on Grant's forces. Troops in great numbers were accordingly hurried to Corinth, and the enemy was preparing to assume the offensive. To counteract this, General Buell's command, numbering nearly 40,000 men, and Buell himself, were ordered from Nashville to the support of General Grant. And there was imminent need of such support. The movements of General Buell, however, were seldom expeditious," &c. (Imminent need of support, March 17, 1862?)

General Sherman informs us, through Colonel Bowman,

"that General Halleck had decided to advance up the Tennessee river as far as practicable by water then to debark on the west bank, attack the enemy at Corinth, and endeavor to cut him off from the east, &c. During the last week of March the Army of the Tennessee only waited for the Army of the Ohio."[1] General Buell had informed General Grant that he would join him before that time. On the morning of the 6th of April the Army of the Ohio had not yet come. The importance of the crisis was apparent, but Buell marched his troops with the same deliberation as " if no other army depended on his promptness." There was imminent need of support, such as Buell's, we are told. The importance of the crisis was apparent, says Sherman; but Buell's march was not altered by the consideration that another army depended upon his promptness.

The apprehension of danger both by Grant and Sherman must be borne in mind as we proceed, as this danger of attack was denied on the 5th of April, 1862. The point here aimed at by this relator is, that if there was imminent need of Buell's support as early as the 17th March, the need increased in proportion of the increase and proximity of the enemy, and, therefore, it was essential that Buell should have had daily or hourly information of the progress of the enemy, in the increase of his force, and his actual or probable approach to the point of danger.

Now, if General Grant had been the man described by Sherman as the second Washington, he would have been the first to repel this charge of tardiness, if for no other reason than that Buell, as he admits, saved him and his army from ruin on the 6th day of April, 1862, at Pittsburgh landing.

It was not the fact that Buell was ordered from Nashville to support Grant. This expression, "to support Grant," is made the origin of all the obloquy thrown upon the former, (Buell,) in not supporting Grant in time to prevent the slaughter and disgrace of April 6, 1862. Buell's Army of the Ohio was ordered over to form a junction with the Army of the Tennessee at Savannah, on the east side of the Tennessee river, nine miles below Pittsburgh,

1. To march on Corinth.

which destination was afterwards altered to Hamburgh, on the west side, after, it is said, General C. F. Smith, on General W. T. Sherman's suggestion, had fixed upon Pittsburgh landing as the best point at which to organize the army to advance on Corinth. The two armies were to be united at Savannah, and when ready to advance with adequate men and means, were to be under the immediate command of Halleck, as happened after the battle.

Halleck was most anxiously striving for the general command of the Union army, vacated on the 11th or 12th of March by the relief of McClellan.

Sherman, stung by his having been deemed unequal to the situation in Kentucky, was madly, but not insanely striving for promotion. But, as will be apparent, with that craftiness which is generally imputed to unfortunates of an unsound mind. Grant was striving, as usual, for any thing chance or Providence might throw in his way, indifferent alike to the intrigues of Sherman or Halleck, so that "profits might accrue" to this "Ancient Pistol" of modern war. All, more or less schemers, were alike striving for individual interest entirely, and were, perhaps, the most successful triumvirate that ever engaged in a combination for the advancement of each other, with regard to nothing else.

An actual design will be proven by comparing the statements above quoted from Bowman and Badeau, on Sherman and Grant, with the actual circumstances existing, and to exist, before, at, and after the battle of Shiloh. This commentary is not intended to be, it is repeated, so much a narrative of events, as the exposition of concealments and the correction of fallacies and fictions, indulged in for selfish purposes by the principal actors and their coadjutors in and out of the army, especially the last.

It will have been seen by the above or previous correspondence, that General Buell would long before have been up the Tennessee, as far as practicable, or to Florence, but for Halleck's ulterior designs as to his own promotion, and to keeping Buell inactive. The whole tending, and intending, to lengthen the war. Grant pretends that there was imminent need of Buell's support on the 17th of March: perhaps from his knowledge that Johnson was forming the junction at Corinth, wanted by Halleck. But he tells Halleck there is no immediate danger, whatever there might have been, here is an extract from his dispatch to Halleck of April 5, 1862, from which it is seen that he says:

"I have scarcely the faintest idea of an attack (general one) being made upon us, but will be prepared should such a thing take place."

Sherman writes to Grant the same day:

"All is quiet along my lines now; we are in the act of exchanging cavalry, according to your orders."

And he adds:

"I have no doubt that nothing will occur today but some picket firing."

It will have been seen by the assertion of Sherman, through Bowman,[2] that Halleck intended to advance up the Tennessee as far as practicable by water. Halleck had said that he so intended, (as we have seen,) to advance as high as Florence, not to cut the enemy off' from the East, as Sherman says, but to cut Johnson off' from the West, which, against Buell's and McClellan's urgency, he concluded not to do, for reasons above intimated, so that the above statement is clearly fallacious.

1st. In impressing the idea that Halleck did advance as to cutting off the enemy far as practicable up the Tennessee; and, 2nd, that the object was to prevent troops going East instead of West; while not a word is said about the failure to occupy Florence, which silence is most significant of the intention and wish, both of Halleck and Sherman, that the rebel junction should take place, so as to provoke a battle outside of Buell's command. "During the last week of March, says Sherman, the Army of the Ohio only waited for the Army of the Tennessee" to march and fight of course. Yet, as will be seen, Sherman reproved Buckland,

---

2. See extract from Bowman, Sherman, &c.

on the 4th of April, for capturing prisoners, whereby an attack might have been brought on before the Army of the Tennessee was ready. (When was it ever ready?)

Sherman also says in his report that many of the troops were unprovided with ammunition, (could they then advance?) There is official evidence that no intrenching tools could be had up to the day of the battle. Could he advance without axes? That Prentiss wanted five regiments to make up his division, and that regiments intended for the march on Corinth arrived on the day of the battle, and many of them not for ten or more days afterwards. The army, Sherman knew, was not to march till General Halleck came up, and further, that on the 28th General Halleck writes that large reinforcements are being sent to General Grant.

Beyond all this, General Halleck, on the 5th of April, dispatches to General Buell that he is right about concentrating at Waynesboro, thirty miles west of Savannah, thus causing delay of one or more days, and says, as usual, that future movements must depend on those of the enemy, and also that he will not be able to leave St. Louis till the 7th or 8th of April, all of which must of course have been known to General Sherman and Grant, as still more cause of delay before the army could march.

Buell, he says, had informed General Grant that he "would join him before the 1st of April." This statement is utterly gratuitous, and little suits the veracity and honour of a soldier. Grant does not claim that he himself fixed a time for Buell to be up. On the 1st of April, Buell dispatches to Halleck that he expects to concentrate at Savannah on the 6th and 7th. This is the first evidence of any time fixed on by Buell, and Grant never named a day for Buell's arrival, as will be seen, before the 7th and 8th; while, as will be proven, he expected the battle of Shiloh would have been fought without Buell, before that date, from the 3rd to the 7th. Again, says Sherman, on the 6th of April, "the Army of the Ohio had not yet come." Now, Sherman knew that Buell's advance division reached Savannah before noon of the 5th, and thus charges General Grant himself with dereliction for not telling him of Buell's arrival, on the evening of that day, the 5th, when he was at Sherman's quarters at Shiloh, late in the afternoon, and remained there, or at his boat at the landing, till near midnight, purposely to avoid meeting Buell, who had requested a meeting that day, April 5th, with Grant, at Savannah, where he (Buell) arrived at 5 p. m., to find Grant not there. Instructions, says Sherman, had been sent by General Grant to expedite Buell's advance and push on to Pittsburgh.

The reverse was the case, and Sherman must have known that, expecting an attack, as he swears he did every hour after the afternoon of the 3rd of April, Grant had not only not countermanded an order sent Nelson, of Buell's army, March 30th, not to he at Savannah before the 7th, but that, on the 4th of April, knowing Nelson to be twenty miles from Savannah, he sent him word that he need not be up till the 8th of April, as he could not ferry him across the river till that time. "The importance of the crisis was apparent," says Sherman, for Johnson would naturally seek to strike Grant before Buell's arrival, and yet he was a party to the attempt, at least twice, to keep Buell back till long after the blow should be struck. Buell, he says further, marched his troops as if no other army depended on his promptitude that is, depended for safety from defeat, of course, on him, (Buell.)

What, then, must be thought of these repeated efforts to keep Buell back till after the expected attack? How could Buell suppose danger possible, when his advance division, under Nelson, was first informed, March 30th, that he was not wanted at Savannah till April 7th; and again, on the 4th of April, when twenty miles off, that he need not be up till the 8th following, or three to five days after? Sherman's own evidence, on oath, shows that he expected the attack on the 3rd, and the worst deception of all for the public, is the statement that Buell caused intervals of six miles to be observed between (the heads of) his divisions: a soldierly arrangement which Sherman habitually neglected, and consequently on a march habitually had his troops in confusion.

Let us examine the wisdom of this arrangement: Say there

were 7,000 men in each division. These would require one and a half miles in line of battle, and over three miles on a route march; and the artillery and trains of an army will, in general, require as much space as the troops, and far more, with such a commander as Sherman or Grant. There was not, however, an average of over 6,000 men, if that, to a division, and the baggage was cut down below the average, so that the six miles so invidiously introduced, as an obvious means of delay, would be barely sufficient to avoid confusion.

There are in a space of one page and two lines of this third chapter of Bowman, on Shiloh, at least fifteen statements such as the above, some of which are noted elsewhere in this treatise, especially that easily exploded fallacy that "Sherman merely made a feint of landing at Eastport." This may have also been done; but, as has been stated, he landed a few miles below, and, marching out in the rain near four miles, effected nothing more than to fatigue and consign hundreds of men to the sick list to endanger the whole division of 8,000 men, and, as his admirer, Draper, says, "to occasion the drowning of many men and horses in the swollen streams." This condition of the streams he also knew would exist when he started, at 2 a. m., on a fifteen or twenty mile trip, the water then rising eight inches an hour.

This characteristic piece of strategy has thus been hushed up, laid on C. F. Smith by Grant, or made a triumphant success by Greeley in the destruction of Burnsville or Corinth, it is hard to say which, from the philosopher's syntax. There are, in this chapter of Sherman's on Shiloh, from pages 47 to 57 inclusive, which, in the above-stated proportion, say on twelve pages, would contain 180 fallacies, suppressions, or fictions. So that, whatever may be this commander's reputation as a tactition and strategist, it is a mere trifle to his archery practice with the long-bow.

The following utterly fallacious, and indeed fictitious, statement of General Grant should not escape attention, though noted elsewhere:

At the battle of Shiloh General Sherman held, on the first day, with raw troops, the key-point of the landing. It is no disparagement to any other officer to pay, that I do not believe there was another division commander of the skill and experience to have done it. (*No one did do it.*)

To his individual efforts I am indebted to the success of that battle. "*Was the 6th a success?*" *W. P. G.* (U. S. Grant.)

Now, not to be in the least critical or disparaging, where these "two mighty warriors" (see sensational history,) are concerned, it may as well be explained, that the key-point of any battle line or any position aimed at beyond it, is that point of approach where the line is easiest pierced, or turned, or entered, for a special purpose. This key-point at Shiloh, should have been the Corinth road at Shiloh church, on Sherman's centre; but Sherman threw away this key-point, by leaving a gap of over a mile on the left of his left centre brigade, near half a mile to the left of the Shiloh church.

This became then not only a key to a closed gate, but an open highway, through which the enemy could march in column by division of a mile front to the flanks and rear of three division of the Union army. There is evidence in this treatise, and in Sherman's report, that near this gap in front of his left centre brigade he was fired on from the thicket in front, his orderly killed, and he instantly and considerately rode rapidly to the rear. The rear, be it understood, being the usual proper place for a commander in action; but he did not stop in rear of this left regiment now doubly left which stood its ground against the example from ten to twenty minutes, and then, making discretion the better part of valour, not only followed the example, but for the time far surpassed the examplar, by a rout in retreat to the landing very early in the fight.

Such is the manner in which, as thousands can prove who were present, Sherman held the key-point to the landing, to which the key had been lost the first day and hour of the battle. As to the results of skill and experience exhibited, the results are the best evidence, as even the benevolent and philosophic Greeley had it impressed on his editorial conviction that Sherman's whole division was scattered at 8 a. m., in which most other writers agree, while they make him the great Horatius at the bridge, of the battle, on the above statement of Grant, quoted from Halleck, who was thereby made commander-in-chief for this single stretch of his long-bow.

As to Sherman's individual efforts in saving the day, reference need only be had to his report, from which it appears he never left his position on the right and rear of McClernand, (to which point he was driven *pell-mell* at 9 or 10 a. m.,) till after the second day's battle. That on the 6th he was driven back to Snake Creek bridge, near three miles north of Shiloh and near two miles west of the landing. So that, by his own report, he could have done nothing in saving the day with the fragments of a few disorganized and disheartened regiments, which did little more than fall back, when threatened, till the end of the battle. But beyond all this, here is General Grant's own report, which, in a little over a year, he seems to have utterly forgotten, or thought worthless:

(Extract,)

Headquarters Division of West Tennessee,
Pittsburgh, April 9, 1862.

The enemy having forced the centre line to fall back nearly half way from their camps to the landing, at a late hour in the afternoon a desperate effort was made by the enemy to turn our left and get possession of the landing, transports, &c. Just at this moment the advance of Major General Buell's column, a part of the division of General Nelson, arrived. The two generals named both being present, (when,) an advance was immediately made upon the point of attack, the enemy was soon driven back.

Now where—"tell us where"—are the personal efforts of General Sherman, out of cannon-shot as he was, at the Snake-creek bridge, waiting for General L. Wallace to come up; and, if Sherman is to be credited, he was, at the time of Nelson's arrival, concluding, with the aid of General Grant, that there had not been "much of a shower after all;" and inasmuch as Lew. Wallace had saved Grant from defeat at Donelson, why should he not do the same next day at Shiloh? Happy and fortunate Lewis Wallace, of the civic crown, who, having had the presumption to attack, without orders, in Grant's absence, for seven or eight hours at Donelson, was fortunately preserved on the 6th for the battle of the 7th. That day, on Sherman's right, he, with McClernand on Sherman's left, literally, as it were, carried along Sherman and his panicked troops through the fight on our right flank. For this and other acts of good soldier-ship at Donelson and Shiloh, these generals were mercifully allowed to command the reserve "in the siege;" perhaps to pick up the shells and stragglers thrown or driven back from that tremendous advance upon, and siege of Corinth, where, as Sherman testifies, Halleck won a victory as brilliant and important as any recorded in history. And who shall doubt such testimony, on authority as undoubtable as this commentary has shown Sherman's evidence to be or not to be that is the question?

P. S. Someone of the earliest Earls of Pembroke, Henry II's time, perhaps, was surnamed Strongbow, from his bold bearing in battle.

If in the approaching imperium simply a question of time there shall be instituted a dukedom for a "Duc de Longebowe," which of these commanders, on their own evidence, should bear the palm, or wear the strawberry leaf on his shoulder-strap or collar?

Chapter 7

How Buell was kept back

General Sherman asked me what was up. I answered, that I had just met and fought the advance of Beauregard's army; that he was advancing on us. Next morning, the 5th, the 5th Ohio cavalry were removed to the 4th division, General Hurlbut. (Major Bicker, 5th O.V. C.)

General Sherman's manner indicated that he was not pleased, as he asked what I had been about. I replied, that I had accidentally got into a little fight, and there were some of the fruits of it, pointing to the prisoners. He answered, that I might have drawn the whole army into a fight before they were ready. (Buckland's Skirmish, April 4, 1862.)

While great stress is, and perhaps ought to be, laid by General Sherman on the fact, that the importance of the crisis was apparent from and after the junction of Johnson and Beauregard at Corinth, about the 20th March, 1862, it is stated that, during the last week of March the Army of the Tennessee only waited for the Army of the Ohio, and at the same time great pains are taken to show that the movements of Buell were seldom expeditious. That, as early as the 16th of March, Halleck had informed Grant that Buell was in motion towards the army at Savannah, Tennessee, and that it took Buell from the 19th of March to the 6th of April, or nineteen days, to march 90 miles; while the writer knew that the march of the 4th (Nelson's) division had been made over this same ground in six days, and Buell himself had ridden it in two days from the evening of the 3rd to the evening of the 5th of April, 1862.

A great effort is also made to prove that while the Army of the Ohio was anxiously expected, exceeding pains were taken to hurry it up; the whole showing, however, being that Grant sent word to McCook, on the 31st March, as follows: "I have been looking for your column anxiously for several days." But no evidence is adduced to prove that any message to that effect ever reached the commander of that army or McCook, or that he was ever advised of any possible immediate danger to the Army of the Tennessee, as he studiously was not so advised.

The statements of Badeau to conceal facts, without seeming to do so, evince much ingenuity, calculated to puzzle and perplex even a professional reader, without due examination. Take, for instance, the following: Grant, he says, had made his arrangements to move his headquarters from Savannah, Tennessee, to Pittsburgh, eight or nine miles above, when a message was brought to him, dated the 4th of April, requesting Grant to remain at Savannah on the 5th, as he (Buell) would arrive there on that day. "I shall be in Savannah myself tomorrow, with perhaps two divisions," said Buell. "Can I meet you there?"

Grant replied, on the 5th: "Your dispatch just received. I will be here to meet you tomorrow, (the 6th.) The enemy at and near Corinth are probably from 60,000 to 80,000."

"Buell, however," says Badeau, "did not arrive till the 6th, or, if otherwise, did not make it known to his superior, and Grant remained to meet him." Now, on the 68th page, behind this statement, we are told that on the 3rd of April Grant was finally able to inform Halleck "that a dispatch from the telegraphic operator is just in. He states that General Nelson, commanding Buell's foremost division, is in sight. The advance will probably arrive on Saturday, the 5th;" but there is ample evidence to prove that Grant did not remain at Savannah all day on the 5th, but avoided meeting Buell that day.

It is notorious that on the morning of the 4th, General Nelson, then twenty miles from Savannah, received a message, stating that he need not hurry his march, and that he could not be ferried over the river before Tuesday, the 8th.

This message of Grant's may have occasioned some delay. But Nelson, an active and impatient commander, did not pay full attention to the dispatch, and his advance, under General Ammen, reached Savannah before noon of the 5th of April, 1862.

Both these divisions, stated by Buell, if hurried, could have been up during the 4th, and McCook's that or next night at furthest.

Crittenden did not get in till on the 6th, at 10 a. m., and then got no orders to go on, but went up of his own accord.

This is the anxious way in which Buell's troops were hurried up. Grant, meantime, had information, that the main body of the enemy left Corinth the night of the 2nd and 3rd of April, and could, as expected, have been at Shiloh the afternoon of the 3rd, had he marched as fast as Grant, the previous February, had done from Fort Henry to Fort Donelson twelve miles in half a day. So says his autobiographer, Badeau. Though the rebel march was delayed till afternoon of the 3rd, there had been since April 1st a large rebel force at Monterey, five miles on the way to Corinth. Sherman has testified under oath that there was reason to expect an attack on the 3rd, and there is ample evidence to prove that he thought there was sufficient force in his front to attack him on the 4th, as follows:

General R. P. Buckland, an especial friend of Generals Sherman and Grant, in describing a picket skirmish on the 4th of April, 1862, says:

"Major Ricker, of the 5th Ohio Cavalry, came up with his cavalry, and we joined in pursuit. We pursued about a mile, when the enemy commenced firing artillery at us. We discovered that he had a large force of cavalry and artillery. We therefore concluded to march back to camp with as little delay as possible. When we reached the picket line General Sherman was there, with several regiments in line of battle. As I rode up to General Sherman, at the head of my column, with about fifteen prisoners close behind me, the General asked me what I had been doing. His manner indicated that he was not pleased. I replied that I had unintentionally got into a little fight, and there were some of the fruits of it, pointing to the prisoners. He answered that I might have drawn the whole army into a fight before they were ready, and ordered me to take my men to camp.

(Yet he (Sherman) swears there was no danger of attack the 4th or 5th.)

Here, then, on the 4th of April, is a clear admission on the part of General Sherman that the enemy, marching from Corinth early the morning of the 3rd, which he thought was the fact, were in full force before him at about 3 or 4 p.m. of the 4th. And an admission, too, of not being ready for an attack, upsetting his assertion in his autobiography by Bowman, that, during the last week of March, the army of the Tennessee only waited for the army of the Ohio to advance upon the rebel force at Corinth. Now, however, it appears that, so far from being ready to advance on the 4th of April, he was not ready to meet an attack in his own lines, if these words to Buckland are worthy of credit. Having given such evidence of what the commanders, Generals Grant and Sherman, thought of a probable attack on the 5th of May, let it be shown what precautions were taken to meet it.

Major Ricker, mentioned above by General Buckland, noticing General Buckland's statement, writes as follows in the *Cincinnati Gazette*, April, 1871:

General Buckland refers to the 5th Ohio volunteer cavalry in his article in the Cincinnati Gazette of April 7, 1871. I propose to give a statement of the part taken by the 2nd battalion 5th Ohio Volunteer Cavalry, for a few days before the battle of Shiloh. From the 24th of March till the 4th of April, the 2nd battalion had almost daily skirmishes with the rebel scouts and pickets. About 3 o'clock p.m.

April 4th, I received an order from General Sherman to go to the front, with one hundred and fifty men, to look for a major, lieutenant, and five or six men, who had wandered outside the lines and were lost or captured.

After relating the occurrence of a sharp skirmish, he proceeds:

Colonel Buckland soon came up with his command on the double-quick. After consultation, we marched back for camp, the 5th Ohio Volunteer Cavalry bringing off eleven prisoners. When we got back to the picket lines, we found General Sherman there, with infantry and artillery in line of battle, caused by the heavy firing of the enemy on us. General Sherman asked me what was up.

I told him I had met and fought the advance of Beauregard's army; that he was advancing on us. General Sherman said it could not be possible. Beauregard was not such a fool as to leave his base of operations at Corinth and attack us in ours.

On Saturday the 5th Ohio Volunteer Cavalry moved their camp to the 4th Division, General Hurlbut. and the 4th Illinois Cavalry took our places with General Sherman's division.

Major Ricker does not state that the 4th Ohio Volunteer Cavalry were moved very early Saturday morning, and that the 4th Illinois Cavalry did not come in till late in the evening of Saturday, the 5th, so that the Union front had no cavalry scouts out that day or night, the 5th.

The object of removing Ricker's cavalry was of course to quiet the suspicions of the enemy as to our alertness on the one hand, and prevent the Union troops from getting information on the other. But not only the cavalry scouts, but three out of the four batteries of Sherman's artillery, were moved back on the morning of the 5th. Two of these batteries were returned at dark to a point eighty rods in rear of Sherman's centre; but that of the second brigade, detached some two miles to the left, was not returned at all, though the position of the brigade was commanded by the heights above Lick Creek, from which this brigade bore the brunt of an artillery attack the morning of the battle. So that, so far as guards and defences were concerned no army was ever more completely exposed to attack than this Army of the Tennessee, till attacked at 6 or 7 o'clock the next day, 6th of April, 1862, utterly unprepared.

Add to this the indications of a battle were never more absolute, whatever the rebel writers may have said about concealing the approach of the attack. At 7 a. m. of the 5th, the pickets opposite the right centre were driven back in three brigades, and the picket stations occupied by the rebel advance less than a mile from the front of the camp.

Early in the afternoon several pieces of rebel artillery were seen at a picket station of the 1st brigade, not three-quarters of a mile in front of the right centre brigade; and all these facts, reported to General Sherman, must have been reported to Grant during the course of the afternoon.

One of the rebel cavalry, wounded on the 4th, and dying during the night, made known that we were to be attacked on the 5th, while at the same time many of the regiments had little or no ammunition for small arms; and the artillery, as next day proved, was yet worse off. Add to this, the camp hospitals were full of men ill with diarrhoea, and men unfit for duty were numbered by the thousand in more than one division, while no regular hospitals had been established at the river.

No intrenching tools, and especially no axes, were to be had, and the colonel of the 46th Ohio, when his regular requisition was reduced and the reduced number not forthcoming, ordered one hundred from Paducah, and the night before the battle got twenty-five—all, he was told, that could be found at Paducah. One hundred axes, properly used for one hour before the attack, would have prevented or defeated it. On such cobweb strands did the lives, and limbs, and liberty of so many thousands hang.

Yet with a knowledge of all these facts, and expecting an attack, known by General Grant to be imminent at any moment, from the myriads of foes gathered and gathering within drum-beat of his front, he dispatches repeatedly to Halleck on the 5th, as follows:

Savannah, April 5, 1862

Major General H. W. Halleck,
    St. Louis, Missouri:

The main force of the enemy is at Corinth, with troops at different points east. Small garrisons are also at Bethel, Jackson, and Humboldt. The number at these places seems continually to change. The number of the enemy at Corinth and within supporting distance of it cannot be far from 60,000 men. Information obtained through deserters places their force west at 200,000. One division of Buell's column arrived yesterday, (the 4th.) General Buell will be here himself today.

        U. S. Grant,   Major General.

The above seems plainly intended to deceive General Halleck. The number of troops (200,000) is intended to keep Halleck away till there are more reinforcements, and the statement about the arrival of Buell's troops the day before is to quiet his apprehensions of an attack without a sufficient Union force. The statement about the troops at and about Corinth is plainly fallacious, as can be proven from a score of sources: he (Grant) knowing these Corinth troops to be within striking distance of his own front. Claiming to know all about troops at Jackson and Humbold, Tennessee, forty to sixty miles off, he cannot deny intimate knowledge of everything at Corinth, but one-third that distance from his front.

Here is another dispatch to Halleck, based on one from Sherman, who says:

Pittsburgh Landing, Tennessee,
April 5, 1862.

General Grant.

Sir: All is quiet along my lines now. We are in the act of exchanging cavalry, according to your orders, and I will send you ten prisoners of war, &c.

W. T. Sherman,   Brigadier General.

Your note yesterday received. I have no doubt that nothing will occur today but some picket firing, &c. I will not be drawn out far, unless with certainty of advantage, and I do not apprehend anything like an attack on our position.

Sherman.

It is to be presumed that with this dispatch at hand Grant telegraphs to Halleck the third time:

Headquarters District of West Tennessee,
Savannah, April 5, 1862.

Major General H. W. Halleck,

St. Louis, Missouri:

Just as my letter of yesterday was finished, notes from General McClernand and Sherman's assistant adjutant general were received, stating that our outposts had been attacked by the enemy, apparently in considerable force. I immediately went up, but found all quiet, &c. They had with them three pieces of artillery and infantry. How much, cannot of course be estimated. I have scarcely the faintest idea of an attack (general one) being made upon us, but will be prepared should such a thing take place.

General Nelson's division has arrived; the other two of Buell's column will arrive tomorrow or next day. It is my present intention to send them to Hamburgh, some four miles above Pittsburgh, when they all get here. Colonel McPherson has gone with an escort today to examine the defensibility of the ground about Hamburgh, &c.[1]

U. S. Grant,   Major General.

Now, to prove what must be more than once repeated, that Grant was deceiving Halleck, by collusion or otherwise, as to occurrences at Pittsburgh, and actually evading Buell, with the same purpose an attack before Buell came up and before repeat-

---

1. McPherson was driven back by the rebel cavalry, which was known to Grant at the time of this dispatch.

ing the occurrences of Saturday, the 5th of April, recurrence must be had to *Badeau's History of Grant*, page 71, in which it is stated that Buell did not arrive till the 6th; or, if otherwise, did not make it known to his superior, and Grant remained to meet him. And in a note on the same page is found the statement, that "Buell's official report states that he arrived at Savannah on the 5th, but Grant was not notified of this, and, consequently, had no suspicion of the fact" (because he was away.)

The very repetition of this statement is plainly intended to hide the fact that Grant evaded Buell, and this evasion of him was necessary to the intention of provoking and meeting the expected attack before the knowledge of his (Buell's) arrival should reach the enemy, and before Buell, aware of the danger, should demand that his troops should be sent forward to Hamburgh, or Pittsburgh, or take them forward himself.

Why put off meeting Buell till the 6th, and perplex the reader, by stating, as Badeau states on page 71, that, while writing to Buell on the 5th that he would meet him on the 6th, he nevertheless remains (see Badeau) to meet him on the 5th, and in the same sentence states that Buell did not arrive till the 6ch, knowing the reverse, as he did.

The whole matter of *Badeau's History* from page 68, where he indicates danger to Grant, March 17th, to page 75, where he announces the attack by Johnson, April 6th, is confusedly mixed, without seeming connection or continuation, and is most ingeniously arranged, so as to perplex even a professional reader of more than usual patience and research. One main object of this commentary is to unfold the design of this medley, intended to cover the effort to deceive Halleck by agreement perhaps, and keep him back at St. Louis; to keep Buell back at Columbia or Waynesboro', and, unaware of danger, to keep all knowledge of Buell's arrival out of reach of Grant's own troops and the enemy: all of which was most skillfully and fortunately done till the object was accomplished, which was an attack by the enemy, which Buell's troops should not be present to repel, but in the repulse of which, if necessary, they might be made available, as they were for the salvation of the Army of the Tennessee in its last extremity. But even this last intention was only adopted, as will be seen, when it was found that, against repeated orders or advice, Buell's advance troops were at Savannah, as the whole might have been, in full time not only to have taken part in a battle on the 6th, but, if sent to Hamburgh on the 5th or 6th, to have captured or dispersed the enemy. This must be repeatedly stated.

Going back to page 70, it will be seen that Grant's headquarters remained at Savannah after sending up McClernand and Smith's divisions, "because," says Badeau, "from there he could more easily communicate with Buell, whose deliberate movements had not yet brought him within supporting distance of the Army of the Tennessee." Grant was very anxious to hurry up Buell, and Buell was very slack in hurrying up, is the plain English of what is here intended by Badeau or by Grant, for they are one in this matter.

On page 68 of *Badeau*, the dates are brought down to the 3rd of April. We are told that on the 19th of March Grant wrote to Buell:

There is every reason to suppose that the rebels have a large force at Corinth and many at other points on the road towards Decatur." But he does not tell Buell that these troops on the road towards Decatur are A. S. Johnson's troops from Decatur, gathering at Corinth.

And this note of the 19th is the last communication spoken of by Badeau from Grant to Buell, till the answer to Buell's note of the 4th of April.

Nor does he tell Buell that he is, as Badeau says he was, apprehensive of an attack on Pittsburgh, and is concentrating his own troops at that threatened locality.

On the 26th of March he tells Halleck,

my scouts are just in with a letter from General Buell, who is yet on the east side of Duck river, detained bridge building;" and the next day, the 27th, he dispatches again to Halleck: "I have no news of any portion of Buell's command being this side of Columbia," but says nothing of danger to the army. On the 31st he writes to Halleck:

Two soldiers from the head of McCook's command came in this evening: some of this command crossed Duck river on the 24th and established guards eight miles out that night.[2]

On the same day, the 31st, he (Grant) sent word to McCook, (not Buell,) "I have been looking for your column anxiously for several days." But no dispatch is mentioned by Badeau to Buell or Nelson two or three days before the 31st, and our biographer may not have found on Grant's order-book such a dispatch, where likely it was never entered or was verbal. Let there be a pause in this relation to say here, that before the 31st Grant must have heard of the concentration of A. S. Johnson's troops at Corinth, whence it had been understood at Shiloh they were to march on Pittsburgh the 1st of April, 1862, or account of Buell's approach. No such anxiety as that expressed to McCook, as above stated, is intimated to Buell or Halleck. On the contrary, immediately after the dispatch to Halleck, of the 27th, stating no news of Buell this side of Columbia, he sends a message to Buell or Nelson, in substance as follows:

Savannah. March 28, 1862

General Nelson,

of Buell's advance Division

You will so time your march to Savannah, Tennessee, as to reach there not before Monday, the 7th of April, as the crowd of troops arriving and to be cared for will make it inconvenient to pay proper attention to so large a body of troops before that date.   U. S. Grant.

It may have also been arranged with Halleck, as a further precaution, to keep Buell back at Waynesboro. For, on the 20th,

---

2. An officer of Sherman's division kept a diary, and on this 31st March, the entry is: "Further indications through the pickets that an attack is imminent, and though I don't fear the result, a sudden attack, if violently made, as it will be, may throw us back for months. The men are discouraged at our delay here, and the close vicinity of the rebel scouts, which should be driven off. Sherman is inviting an attack, for which we are unprepared, but which I hope may occur."

Halleck writes that Buell is "marching on Waynesboro," there to concentrate and march thence to Hambugh, four miles above Pittsburg. "From that point to Corinth the road is good, and a junction can be formed with the troops from Pittsburgh at almost any point." (Grant to Halleck, Savannah, April 5, 1862.)

It was intended by Nelson not to reach Savannah before the 7th, and Buell expected a dispatch at Waynesboro to stop him there. But by some fatality Nelson had just passed Waynesboro when Buell got there, and, meeting no dispatch from Halleck, Buell pushed on to Savannah, reaching there at 5 p. m. on the 5th.

Grant's combinations to defeat 100,000 rebels with less than half their supposed number had miscarried. The affair, as sailors say, had missed stays; and, says Colonel Adam Badeau,

> On the 3rd of April Grant was finally able to inform Halleck that, according to the telegraphic operator, General Nelson, commanding Buell's foremost division, is in sight. (From what station?) The advance will arrive, probably, on Saturday, April 5th, (*when Grant kept purposely away. W. P. G.*)

Now, here is a blunder, real or intended, calculated to befog the casual and perplex or irritate the professional reader. Why say a body of troops in sight on the 3rd, or even the 4th of April, will only "probably arrive on the 5th," when so anxiously expected? The country about Savannah, in the direction of Waynesboro, was level and wooded, and a mile was probably the limit of vision in that direction. The inference may be, what was probably the fact, that Nelson might act upon the message from Grant of the 4th, that he need not hasten his march; and there was, therefore, room for such a probability. But this dispatch, at least, proves, outside the message to Nelson, that no effort was made to have Nelson up in time to defend the attack Grant and Sherman knew was intended to be made on or about the 5th, and of which, with no other evidence than that of Buckland and Kicker, above stated, Sherman on the 4th felt certain of on the 5th.

These messages or dispatches, endeavouring to delay Buell's arrival, if ever reduced to writing, or placed upon record, with numbers of others, incriminating both Grant and Halleck in regard to their own and Buell's operations about this time, have doubtless been suppressed, and, as such messages may seem surprising to readers knowing little or nothing of the parties here concerned, the following evidence maybe of interest to all concerned, especially old volunteers of these armies:

Cincinnati, February 12, 1872

I was in command of the 10th brigade, 4th division, (General W. Nelson commanding division,) army of the Ohio, on its march from Nashville to Savannah, Tennessee, in the spring of 1862.

On leaving Columbia, Tennessee, about the last of March, General Nelson directed me to conduct the march, so as to reach Savannah, Tennessee, the 7th of April, as we were not wanted there before.

The roads were good, the weather pleasant, and camping grounds favourable, which will account for our reaching Savannah before noon April 5th, 1862. If required, the march might have been hastened without fatigue to the troops or leaving any part of the train behind.

J. Ammen.

Supposing it plain now that, while anxiously seeming to expect Buell, Grant was still more anxiously striving to keep him back, the text of Colonel Badeau is again taken up.

CHAPTER 8

How Grant was Prepared the Night Before the Battle

General Grant, while at Springfield, Massachusetts, said that Buell might have reached Pittsburgh landing several days earlier than he did, in which case General Grant would have been the attacking party. (*N.Y. Herald,* August, 1865.)

It is exceedingly convenient, especially for a military man or historian, to forget, or omit, or misplace dates, which are generally of the utmost importance, even to a minute or a second of time, during or before a battle, and are important at all times. General Grant's report of Shiloh proves that five minutes' more delay might have lost his army. The enemy on our extreme right, on the 6th of April, 1862, about noon, failed to turn that flank by withholding his fire in a single instance not over a second of time. Our biographer, whether prompted or not, takes advantage of this circumstance to omit or confuse his dates as emergencies seem to require. Thus we are told that a message from Buell, dated April 4th, was brought to Grant, not stating whether received the 4th or 5th. Grant replies on the 5th, at Savannah: "Dispatch just received; I will be here to meet you tomorrow. The enemy at and near Corinth are probably from 60,000 to 80,000."

"And," says Badeau, "Buell, did not arrive till the 6th, and Grant remained to meet him."

Now, if the writer of this mixed matter intended to say that

Grant retained his headquarters at Savannah to meet Buell, he should so specify. But Grant's headquarters were, or were supposed to be, on the boat Tigress, while his adjutants had offices on shore, both at Pittsburgh and Savannah. The fate of two armies of 80,000 men depended in a great measure on the meeting of these two commanders. And here was one most anxiously expected, as we are told, while the other, in the utmost danger, as the event proved he was and professed to be, not only endeavours to keep his troops back, but delays an answer to a dispatch received on the 4th of April till the 5th; and writing on the 5th, which, it is repeated, was the last limit of the expected attack, he postpones the requested interview to the 6th, and by this he plainly postpones this requested meeting until after the attack did come, as was expected; and, but for several accidents of the most improbable character, this postponement must have been more fatal to both armies than the delay was to the one so miraculously saved, and then thrown back, as it was, at any rate, one to two months in its expected operations.[1]

Consider again this confusion of dates, which is repeated two pages forward, (page 73.) Grant writes to Buell on the 5th: "I will be here to meet you tomorrow, the 6th."

"Buell did not arrive till the 6th, and Grant remained to meet him," says Badeau.

When? On the 5th, when this answer was written, or the day after? Now, it is certain that General Grant saw General Nelson soon after noon on the 5th, and must have heard from him of the proximity of General Buell. He also sees Colonel Ammen; tells him he is not wanted, as he does not expect a fight much outside of Corinth. Knowing that General Buell will be at Savannah on the 5th; and, expecting every moment to hear the roar of an attack above, he runs up in the Tigress, after seeing Nelson, to Pittsburgh, and does not return till near midnight, and thus avoids seeing Buell.

Next morning, roused up by the roar of rebel cannon, he hastily and forgetfully writes to Buell as follows: "Savannah,

---

1. This was the object of the Washington cabal. W. P. G.

April 6, 1862. Heavy firing heard up the river, indicating an attack on my most advanced position. I expected this, but did not think it would take place till tomorrow or next day," (Monday or Tuesday, 7th or 8th.)

And this is written after he had dispatched to Nelson at Columbia that he was not wanted till the 7th, written after he had arranged with Halleck to stop Buell, to close up at Waynesboro, (thirty miles off,) and march thence to Hamburgh; after advising Nelson on the 4th that he would be in the way if up before the 8th; and after saying to General Ammen that his troops were thus superfluous, as he did not expect a fight much short of Corinth, telling him to hold to the position he was in till boats came down for him; and then, as Colonel Badeau relates, ordering Nelson, with extreme providence, to move to a point five miles below Pittsburgh, forgetting, of course, the previous order to Ammen, to remain where he was—at Savannah.

And this is the greatest soldier of the age, honest and just, as a man should be! This then, is the provident commander, who had been so anxious for Buell's arrival over a week before the 5th! Buell who, as Sherman says and swears, had been rightfully expected for two weeks; and therefore he (Sherman) maintained the gaps in our front for an army which was to go elsewhere, but knew their real use was gates to the enemy in cannon-shot of our camps, and whose entry thereat was by him so successfully repelled, if any faith is to be placed in his letter to Professor Coppes, contradicting his division report, written immediately after the battle. Buell, be it repeated, was not sent to Hamburgh, as he would have prevented the attack. But to return again to Colonel Badeau's dates, jumbled together like a crate of dates, and confused as the bloody battle about to break upon and break to pieces the Army of the Tennessee.

After the statement that on the 5th Grant remained to meet Buell at Savannah, a very free use is made of that day, the 5th, which may here be taken for either the 5th or 6th. It will be seen, however, very plainly, that he did not remain on the 5th, the day fixed by Buell to see him. He remained there, however, long enough to meet Nelson and Ammen, and give them conflicting orders, which came very near, say within five or ten minutes, of utterly scattering or capturing the Army of the Tennessee, late in the afternoon of the 6th, when, it is again repeated, as is stated in Grant's report, these rejected troops of Buell's, under Nelson and Ammen, prevented the turning of our extreme left and the capture of the landing, transports, &c., while so near the army to be deserted by Grant. But to the dates again:

> There was skirmishing daily after the 2nd of April, and on the 4th the enemy felt Sherman's front in force, but nothing serious came of it, and the opinion of that commander was, that no probability of an immediate engagement existed. (Though there had been danger three weeks before.) Grant rode out on the day after, i. e., the 5th, and concurred with him in this judgement.

Now, supposing, of course, that these commanders, in good faith, put these words out of or into the pen of their biographer, what is to be thought of them as men above idiocy, to say nothing of their being commanders, intrusted at the time with the destinies of two large armies, quadruple in number that with which the great Julius won the empire of the olden world at Pharsalia?

Consider the circumstances then, by them known to exist, as has never been denied. Sherman and Grant both believed the enemy had marched from Corinth the night of the 2nd and 3rd; a very large force having been in our front for some days before. Sherman has testified that there was reason to expect an attack on the 3rd, and Grant has admitted that he thought an army equal to his own on the evening of that day (the 3rd) was in his front. Johnson marched on the 3rd, so as to attack before Buell came up, as arranged by Grant, on the 7th or 8th: he (Johnson) having fixed early on the 5th for the attack.

How it was possible he failed to know that Buell's advance was at Savannah the 5th, at noon, who can conjecture; but such ignorance, on some reliable assurance, must have existed. Our commanders now (the 5th) recognized how close the chances were of his retreat or his attack, and Beauregard advised a withdrawal of his troops. Grant had been assured on the 4th that Buell's advance was in sight of the station, and Buell himself, Grant knew, was to be on the ground with two divisions that day, (5th.) On the 4th of April, 1862, the day before these commanders concurred in their judgement, says Badeau, against the probability of an immediate attack, Sherman had been assured by Major Bicker that he had just met the advance of Beauregard's army, and Sherman had admitted it by telling Buckland that, by capturing prisoners, he might have drawn our whole army into a fight before they were ready. But beyond this the meeting of Grant and Sherman must have been late in the afternoon of the 5th. Badeau admits this imminent attack, by stating Grant's orders to Nelson as to placing his camp five miles from Pittsburgh on the 5th.

Grant then went up late on the 5th for two very special reasons. One was to avoid meeting Buell, and let Sherman know how close the chances were, and to prevent all possible information to the enemy, for which reason the cavalry pickets had been withdrawn the night before, (4th.) They had both known or believed that an advance in force had been within the power of the enemy since 2 p. m. of the day before, (the 4th,) or even the 3rd, and were no doubt in extreme apprehension that, knowing Buell's proximity, the rebels had retreated, or determined so to do that night, as some advised.

But, more than all this, there had occurred that day what Sherman and Grant concealed in their reports—what they seem, according to Badeau; to have concealed even from Halleck, (and what they have seemingly or actually concealed from Badeau and Bowman, which is left in doubt)—occurrences not mentioned in the dozen histories and thousands of accounts of the battle, and obtained by Colonel Worthington's court-martial in August, 1862. At 7 a. m. (5th) the pickets of the 1st brigade were driven in from a station three quarters of a mile, as Sherman testifies, from his right centre, and soon after the pickets of the two centre brigades were also driven back. The 5th April, early in the afternoon, one or more rebel guns were in battery at this picket station of Sherman's 1st brigade, and rebel artillery was heard of farther to our left, opposite Shiloh Church, and reported to Sherman, who had no guns at hand.

The woods in front swarmed all day with rebel troops of all arms, as Colonel (now General) Buckland testified, and mentions in his letter to the Cincinnati Gazette, indicating the power to attack and warning the immediate approach of the enemy.

These facts are here repeated as known to Grant on the 5th, in the afternoon, when he avoided meeting Buell; and to prove that he did this purposely, (see Ammen's note, &c., above.) He thus kept Buell back, knowing himself liable at any moment to attack, while he kept his front exposed and defenceless. Yet this charge has been and is sneered at as a queer idea, that any general of any army should commit such an act of folly, or madness, or criminality, whatever be its denomination in the calendar of crime, or of insanity, or selfish purpose, or interest. The very confusion and omission of dates now in hand prove the design charged by the avoidance of Buell on the 5th.

We have it stated, after mention of this interview between Grant and Sherman on the 5th, that on the 4th "Grant's horse slipped and fell on his rider. This lamed him for over a week," &c. This fall, and especially the lameness, was not apparent on the 6th to anybody, and was never known to this narrator till seen in *Badeau's history*. The report may have been spread as an additional inducement to the attack, and Grant's going every night to Pittsburgh was calculated to lull the suspicion of the enemy that their attack was expected, and to quiet any apprehension in his own army.

But this accident of the 4th should have been stated in its place—not so stated as to produce the impression that the concurrence of judgement was on the 4th. He keeps on mixing dates. The same day, we are to infer, on which Grant got hurt, the 4th, Lew. Wallace reported eight regiments of rebel infantry and 1,200 cavalry at Purdy, &c.; and the same day, the 4th, he

(Grant) writes to Sherman:

> "I will return to Pittsburgh landing tomorrow, (the 5th,)
> at an early hour," &c.

An interview between Grant and Sherman on the 5th has
been noticed at length by Badeau. If he did go up in the forenoon, he was back at Savannah at noon and some hours later;
and, going up to Pittsburgh in the afternoon to avoid Buell, his
impressions as to an immediate attack must have been the same;
and it is a fair presumption that Badeau was made aware of all
that occurred at Shiloh as to pickets, and before Grant returned
to Savannah at 11 p. m. that night, or so much pains would not
be taken to explain this avoidance of Buell on the 5th.

We come now to Saturday, April 5th, and will be done with
these tedious and tangled dates—tangled at a time when of all
others they should be eminently straight and clear. On Saturday,
April 5th, Sherman is quoted to show that the enemy's cavalry came down well to his front, and what is stated before by
Badeau is repeated. It is repeated that Grant, having made all his
preparations to remove his headquarters to Pittsburgh on the
morrow, (the 6th,) remained to meet Buell, as that "officer had
desired, on the 5th."

The inference here is plain, that Grant remained in person
to meet Buell on the 5th, as Buell had desired, (on page 70.) To
which desire on the 5th (page 71) Grant writes: "I will be here
to meet you tomorrow."

Buell, however, says Badeau, did not arrive till the 6th, and
Grant remained to meet him. If there is any doubt about the date
specified or meant by Badeau here, there can be none where this
same matter is specified (page 73) as a meeting on the 5th, as
Buell had desired.

A battle may be lost by delay or precipitation; by blundering or neglect; by misinformation or by accident, as thousands
of battles have been lost or won, and yet the delinquent general
may preserve his honour, and even his reputation. Soult never
won a battle, and was beaten repeatedly, and especially and un-

expectedly by what seemed, and may have been, a blunder, at Albuera, but lost no reputation; while Beresford, who won the battle, gained none. Yet though Beresford was chargeable with neglect of the same sort as that at Shiloh, both he and Soult did all of which their minds and means were competent, neglected no reinforcements that could be got up before the battle, and made the best use they could of their troops in hand: they themselves all the time remaining on the battlefield. Soult blundered in his tactics; and Beresford, it is said, lost his temper on the field of "Albuera, lavish of its dead;" almost as Shiloh. But neither of these generals was charged or chargeable with designed neglect, or a selfish purpose, and their honour was not tarnished.

But here is a case where an endeavor was plainly made to delay the approach of much-needed reinforcements to the aid of a threatened army, and, what is worse, an absolute rejection occurs of the anxiously expected troops when arrived, and when an attack was momentarily expected, and when these troops, if used as had been intended, could have crushed their adversaries in an hour, or one-fourth the time, if properly handled. And though ten years have passed, there has been no suspicion expressed but by this relator, that any one but General Buell was in fault, and, by his deliberation, was the cause of the slaughter and disgrace at Shiloh, April 6, 1862. Hoping we have hunted down these dates with a legitimate purpose to expose their nefarious use, and hunted up and out their concealment and confusion to an understanding of the fact, that while, as is pretended, Grant remained to meet Buell on the 5th of April, 1862, he purposely avoided doing so:—the tedious detail may not be without interest and instruction to a professional reader;

The following letter, to show whether intentionally or not the meeting with Buell was avoided, is introduced.

Grant and Sherman admit, by Grant's dispatch to Halleck, that they had not the faintest idea of an immediate attack on the 5th., there was nothing, then, to keep Grant from Savannah on the 5th, where he had remained, we are told, for the purpose of hurrying forward Buell's troops. We are here shown how he did it, by remaining at Pittsburgh, knowing Buell to be at Savannah:

August 27, 1862

My statement of where I was and what I was doing April 5th and 6th, (1862,) is as follows:

I was sent in charge of ten prisoners and ten guards to Pittsburgh landing from Shiloh meeting-house by Colonel Hildebrand, commanding 3rd brigade, on Saturday, April 5th. The prisoners had been taken the day before, and belonged to companies C, K, and D, of 1st Alabama cavalry. On Saturday evening I was ordered by General U. S. Grant to put my men all on board the steamer Tigress, with one day's rations, and take the prisoners to Savannah that night. We landed at Savannah about 11 p. m., and General Grant said it was not advisable to take the men ashore that night. He, with other officers, remained up to a very late hour, and were very late in getting up on Sunday morning.

I finally got an order to take the prisoners to the guard-house, and was told my guards might remain in town till 4 p. m. At that time the boat was to start back to Pittsburgh landing. I had just got to the guard-house when I heard cannonading in the direction of Shiloh. I looked down towards the steamboat landing, and saw that the *Tigress* was. firing up. I took my men (the guards) back on double-quick, and scarcely got there in time to get on board the boat. General Grant stayed all night on the boat. We halted at Crump's Landing, and Grant inquired of Commodore ———— where the firing was at. Answer, 'in Sherman's division.' Grant remarked, 'I would rather it was there than any place else along the line, for he is better prepared for them.' He then ordered the boat on up to Pittsburgh, at which place we arrived near 10 o'clock, a. m.

E. R. Moore,
Second Lieutenant Company D, 77th Regiment O. V. I."

If Badeau writes on Grant's authority, that commander indicated his expectation of an attack both by the order (which we are told was obeyed by Nelson) to encamp five miles below Pittsburgh, and by telling Ammen to stay where he was, and that, if wanted, he would send boats down for him; and, therefore, he must have been in momentary expectation of an attack, instead of the attack on the 7th or 8th he told Buell he had been expecting. With all this expectation of an attack on the 7th, there is no accounting for the fact, that he did not send Buell's troops up on Saturday, except by the conclusion that he purposely kept him back to prevent his having any share in the expected repulsion of an attack. With Sherman the purpose might have been different, if, as he had said, his heart was not in the war.

On page 72 we are told that the skirmish of the 4th put both officers and men on the alert. We have seen, that among these officers were not Sherman and Grant. Sherman parked his two centre batteries eighty rods in rear of his centre on the evening of the 5th, and told a large number of troops, who were on the lookout near Shiloh church after dark, to disperse to their quarters, where they would be in no more danger than if at home in Ohio. Suppose, now, these commanders had been upon the alert, and, as was dispatched to Halleck on the 5th, had been ready to meet an unexpected attack, would not the threatening occurrences of Saturday, the 5th, have been dispatched hourly, or oftener, to Halleck and to Buell's troops in the rear? Would not notice have been sent to Buell so soon as the pickets were driven in at 7 a. m.? Would not boats have been ready to take up the division of Nelson that arrived at noon on the 5th? Would not Grant's scattered divisions have been warned of the danger, and the widely separated columns have been brought into regular line of battle that threatening afternoon and day?

Sherman may perhaps be excused for inaction on the ground of his theory that fortifications would have been a sign of weakness, and invited an attack, for which he was not ready on the 4th, or 5th, or 6th, or ever in the war. Drawing his lines up so as to close the gaps, and properly arranging his artillery on the front or flanks, would, on the same principle, have incurred the temptation to attack; and to lead even an enemy into temptation of shedding blood, would have been morally and religiously wrong, and so he remained inactive, lest he might induce an attack for which we were not prepared. Such inactivity, in addition to the presentation of his flanks to an expected attack, is the new Shermanic strategy.

CHAPTER 9

Sherman's Evidence

Extract from record of court martial at Memphis, Tennessee, August, 1862.

No stronger position was ever held by any army. Therefore on Thursday, (3rd of April,) two days before the battle, I knew there was no hostile force within six (three) miles, though there was reason to expect an attack. The diary entry that an attack was imminent on Thursday, April 3, 1862, is false and libellous. (Sherman's evidence.)

We did not occupy too much ground. General Buell's forces had been expected rightfully for two weeks, and a place was left for his forces, though Grant had afterwards determined to send Buell to Hamburgh as a separate command. The entry that we covered too much ground is false and libelous. (Sherman's evidence.)

Extracts from the record of Colonel Worthington's trial at Memphis, Tennessee, August, 1862:

EXTRACTS FROM A DIARY OF THE TENNESSEE
EXPEDITION, 1862, BY T. WORTHINGTON,
COLONEL 46TH REGIMENT, O.V. I.

Wednesday, *March 26, 1862.*—At Camp Shiloh, three miles from Pittsburgh landing. A company being called for picket duty today, detailed Captain Sharp's company, B. Indications of an attack, if the country people are to be believed. Their pickets are around, and too near us, showing a strong effective force.

Thursday, *March 27, 1862.*—This afternoon two of Sharp's pickets were fired on by the rebel horse, about 4 p.m., not a mile from camp. A disgrace to the army that such should be the case, and an indication that they are covering some forward movement, yet Sherman is improvident as ever, and takes no defensive and scarce any precautionary measures. He snubs me, and has no time to hear even a suggestion.

Friday, *March 28, 1862.*—Having suggested to McDowell the sending out if a stronger picket, he ordered thirty more men, which were immediately volunteered. if Beauregard does not attack us, he and the chivalry are disgraced forever, if for nothing else.

Saturday, *March 29, 1862.*—Sherman has refused to sign a requisition for seventy-two axes for my regiment, making it twenty-two; and while a slight abattis might prevent or avert an attack, there are no axes to make it, nor is there a sledge or crowbar in his division, and scarce a set of tools out of my regiment.

Monday, *March 31, 1862.*—Further indications through the pickets that an attack is imminent, and though I do not fear the result, a sudden attack, if violently made, as it will be, may throw us back for months. The men are discouraged at our delay here and the close vicinity of the rebel pickets, which should be driven off. Sherman is inviting an attack, which I hope may occur, but for which we are unprepared.

Tuesday, *April 1, 1862.*—Have now over one hundred rounds of ammunition for all available men, and feel easy on that point. Ordered the captains to send in accounts of clothing, &c., wanted, which the quartermaster is very careless about getting. Still no axes, which now he cannot get if he would, and which are worth more than guns at present.

Thursday, April 3, 1862.—Rode to Pittsburgh landing. The place is crowded and in disorder below, with noise and gambling on the bank above, across the way from the post office. Hunted up and down for clothing and axes, and found that Sherman had forbidden his quartermaster from receiving any thing; that General Smith's quartermaster will answer no requisitions outside of his immediate command and the post quartermaster, Baxter, (Grant's,) will only answer the requisitions of the division quartermasters. The reason that Sherman's quartermaster will not receive any stores is, that he has no place to put them.

There are now at least six boats hired by the day at the landing, (as I hear,) at no less than two thousand ($2,000) a day, when two thousand dollars with that many men could, in ten days or less, put up store-houses sufficient for an army of one hundred thousand men. And so the Government will pay on this expedition so far not less than twenty thousand dollars, and perhaps ten times that before the war is over, and lose not less than one to ten million dollars in quartermaster and commissary stores, occasioned by the improvidence and neglect of its major generals here, to say nothing of the disorder and danger growing out of such a state of things.

The indications are (still) of an attack, which I have also intimated to McDowell; we should now have on our right at least six batteries, and two regiments of cavalry to warn the rear. With thick woods .before us and pickets scarce a mile out, we have no defences whatever, and no means of giving an alarm but by the fire of musketry. The troops cover too much ground, and cannot support each other, and a violent attack, which we may expect, may drive them back in detail. God help us, with so many sick men in camp, if we are attacked, there being over five thousand unfit for duty.

Friday, *April 4, 1862.*—One of McDowell's pickets was shot in the hand about noon. A detail of Taylor's cavalry was sent out three or four miles; found four to six hundred rebel cavalry, and fell back, returning about 2 p.m.

Everything is carried on in a very negligent way, and nothing but the same conduct on the other side can save us from disaster. They can concentrate one hundred thousand men from the heart of rebeldom, and with three or four railroads have far greater facilities for handling troops than we have.

Have brigade orders to stack arms at daylight till farther orders. Keep two companies lying on their arms, and though as quiet as possible, look for an attack every hour.

Saturday, *April 5, 1862.*—Rode out to Sharp's pickets at sunrise, and found two men (rebel pickets) wounded yesterday, who died last night at the Widow Howell's. About 7 o'clock a.m., the rebels drove in Lieutenant Crary from the Widow Howell's, getting possession of their dead men. Heard in the evening that the rebels had established three guns (six pounders) opposite Hildebrand's brigade, on our left, across the valley. Hear of five of their regiments arriving today.

Sunday, *April 6, 1862.*—A clear cool morning. Rode out to the pickets at sunrise, and soon after the enemy were seen advancing past the Howell house. Directly one of Colonel Hicks's regiment, 40th Illinois, was shot through the heart, at not less than four hundred yards. Rode to McDowell's quarters, (not up,) and then back to the pickets, and ordered the men who had fallen back to advance to the Howell fence. Returned to camp for preparation, and at about 7 a.m. the attack commenced on Hildebrand's and Buckland's brigades. This might have been expected, but we were really not ready for a fight. No hospitals at Pittsburgh, nor even means to carry off the wounded."

April 25, 1862.

The undersigned hereby certify that most of the facts above set forth are correct from their own knowledge, and that Colonel Worthington's remarks and anticipations are in correspondence with his general conversation for ten days before the battle of the 6th of April, 1862.

> William Smith, Maj. 46th Reg. O.V.I.
> J. W. Heath, Capt. Co. A, 46th Reg. O.V.I.
> A. G. Sharp, Capt. Co. B, 46th Reg. O.V.I.
> Jno. Wiseman, Capt. Co. C, 46th Reg. O.V.I.
> Ed. N. Upton, Lt. Cd'g. Co. D, 46th Reg. O.V.I.
> Wm. Pinney, Capt. Co. E, 46th Reg. O.V.I.

P. A. Crow, Capt. Co. G. 46th Reg. O.V. I.
M. C. Lilly, Capt. Co. H, 46th Reg. O.V. I.
C. C. Lybland, Capt. Co. I, 46th Reg. O.V. I.
I. N. Alexander, Capt. Co. K, 46th Reg. O.V. I.

3rd Charge.—Conduct unbecoming an officer and a gentleman.

Specification 2nd.—In this, that the said Colonel Thomas Worthington, of the 46th Ohio Volunteers, did print, or cause to be printed, on a sheet for circulation, what purported to be extracts from his diary of the Tennessee expedition, containing false and libelous matter, calculated and designed to injure his superior officers, Colonel McDowell and General Grant and General Sherman.

Specification 3rd.—In this, that the said Colonel Worthington did print, or cause to be printed, for circulation, what purported to be extracts from his diary of the Tennessee expedition, designed to secure for himself a popular reputation for prophecy and foresight, while said diary was not made contemporaneous with the dates set forth in it, but was fabricated or manufactured after the occasion, to fulfil some base and dishonourable purpose.

To which the prisoner pleaded not guilty.

General Sherman's testimony, having direct reference to the charges, was as follows:

As to the 3rd charge, 2nd specification, he says, of these facts I can testify, that, about the 10th instant, (August, 1862,) one of my staff brought a sheet of printed matter, which was left for me by Captain Giesy, of the 46th Ohio. That sheet contains matter false and libelous. Though marked private and confidential, it bears on its face evidence of its intent for circulation. Under date of March 29, 1862, by this paper, he uses the words: 'Sherman has refused to sign a requisition for seventy-two axes for my regiment making it twenty-two.' I did so rightfully. I knew what axes were on hand and expected, and was the judge, not Colonel Worthington, of their distribution. (There were none to be had.)

He says, 'a slight abattis might have prevented an attack.' What business was it of his whether his superior officer invited an attack or not? The Army Regulations will show him that no fortifications can be made except under order of the commanding general, (thus making Grant responsible.) To have erected fortifications would have been evidence of weakness and would have invited an attack. The entry of March 31, 1862, must have been fabricated after the date, for our squadrons, regiments, and brigades were on the ground five days after this entry was made. Colonel Worthington might have thought an attack imminent, because for weeks he was predicting the worst, and hoping it might happen.

The entry of April 3, 1862, is false and libelous. Troops were arriving from every quarter by water; wagons were coming to the landing from camps in the interior; high water contracted the levée to a very small space, and many other causes, well known to Colonel W., produced confusion, which no general could have prevented, and which no one could charge to General Grant. (Nothing was charged to General Grant.)

I admit that Colonel Worthington was wandering up and down the river hunting for clothing and axes, but the assertion that Sherman had forbidden his quartermasters to receive anything is an absurdity, (but nevertheless a fact, as is proven.) Now, in this connection, while Colonel Worthington was wandering up and down after axes, I will show what the men in front were doing.

Here follows a statement of scoutings on the 2nd and 3rd of April, in which nothing but rebel cavalry was encountered. He then proceeds to testify as follows:

And here I mention for future history, that our right flank was well guarded by Owl and Snake creeks, our left by Lick creek, leaving us simply to guard our front. No stronger position was ever held by an army. Therefore, on Thursday, two days before the battle, when Colonel Worthington was so apprehensive, (for his personal safety,) I knew there was no hostile party within six (three) miles, though there was reason to expect an attack, (that day.) I suppose Colonel McDowell, like myself, had become tired of his constant prognostications and paid no attention to him, especially when we were positively informed by men like Buckland, Kilby Smith, and Major Ricker who went to the front to look for enemies, instead of going to the landing, (for axes to save his men from slaughter.)

And here I will state, that Pittsburgh landing was not chosen by General Grant, but by Major General Smith. I received orders from General Smith, and took post accordingly; so did General Hurlbut; so did his own division. The lines of McClernand and Prentiss were selected by Colonel (now General) McPherson. I will not insult General Smith's memory by criticizing his selection of a field. It was not looked to so much for defence, as for ground on which our army could be organized for offence.

We did not occupy too much ground. General Buell's forces had been expected rightfully for two weeks, and a place was left for his forces, although General Grant afterward had determined to send Buell to Hamburgh as a separate command.

But even as we were (without defence) on the 6th of April, you might search the world over and not find a more advantageous field of battle—flanks well protected, and never threatened; troops in easy support; timber and broken ground giving good points to rally; and the proof is, that 43,000 men, of whom at least 10,000 ran away, held their ground against 60,000 chosen troops of the South, with their best leaders. On Friday, the 4th, nor officer nor soldier, not even Colonel Worthington, looked for an attack, as I can prove.

On Friday, April 4th, our pickets were disposed as follows: McDowell's brigade, embracing Worthington's regiment, looked to Owl creek bridge, and had nothing to do with any other road. Buckland and Hildebrand covered our line to the main Corinth road. Pickets, one company to a regiment, were thrown forward a mile and a half to the front, *videttes* a mile farther, making a chain of sentinels.

About noon of that day Buckland's adjutant came to my tent and reported that a lieutenant and seven men of his guard had left their post and were missing: probably picked up by a small cavalry force which had hovered around for some days, and which I had failed to bag. I immediately dispatched Major Ricker, with all my cavalry, in a tremendous rain, to the front. Soon after I heard distant musketry, and finally three cannon shots, which I knew must be the enemy, as we had none there.

This was the first positive information any intelligent mind on that field had of any approaching force. Before that, no scout, no officer, no responsible man had seen an infantry or artillery soldier nearer than Monterey, (five miles out.) For weeks and months we had heard all sorts of reports, just as we do now. For weeks old women had reported that Beauregard was coming, sometimes with 100,000, sometimes with 300,000; when, in fact, he did not leave Corinth until after even Colonel Worthington had been alarmed for (his) safety.

As soon as I heard the cannon I and my staff were in the saddle and off for the front. We overtook a party of Buckland's and Hildebrand's brigades going forward to the relief of the pickets. On reaching a position in advance of the guard-house, a mile and a half from Shiloh, they deployed into line of battle, and I awaited the return of my cavalry and infantry, still to our front.

Colonel Buckland and Major Ricker soon returned, and reported encountering infantry, artillery, and cavalry near the fallen timber?, six miles (three miles) in front of our camp. We then knew that we had the elements of an army in our front, but did not know its strength or destination. The guard was strengthened, (not the fact,) and as night came on we returned to camp, and not a man in the camp but knew we had an enemy to the front before we slept that night. But even I had to guess its purpose. No general could have detected or reported the approach of an enemy more promptly than was done, (on that occasion.)

(Here was read a letter of General Sherman to General Grant, dated April 5th, 1862, giving an account of the affair as above stated.)

Thus, while Buckland's brigade, in the execution of its proper duty, was guarding safely our front, a colonel of another brigade, in a safe corner, was looking for an attack every hour, (*probably every minute. W. P. G.*)
As to the journal entry of April 5th, I have but little to say. As to the three guns on Hildebrand's left, he could have heard no such thing, for our troops crossed and recrossed the ground all day Saturday, (*and, as will be seen, reported the artillery. W. P. G.*)
I say it was impossible for him to have heard as to the three guns on our left across the valley. The position is well-known, and was within our pickets. (Fact.) If he heard so, it was his sworn and bounden duty to have reported the fact to his commander, which he did not do. (He says he was tired of such reports.)

Here follow personal reflections on Colonel Worthington, and imputations of publishing foolish reports of Shiloh, little dreaming, he continues, "that one who knew so well would do so much," &c., and closes by saying,

I have given a history of events during the week preceding the battle of Shiloh, and state further, that from the 31st March to the 2nd of April, with part of my division, I was up the Tennessee river to Eastport. From the 2nd to the 7th of April I have given an account. On the 8th of April my division pursued the enemy over the same ground six miles. On the 9th, 10th, and 11th of April I was up the Tennessee and broke the Bear Creek bridge, the original object of the expedition[1] I therefore repeat, that my command did neglect no proper precautions, but was as industrious, and vigilant, and patient as any part of the troops constituting the Army of the Tennessee.

(*The diary extracts were applicable to the management of the whole of the Army of the Tennessee. W. P. G.*)

SHERMAN'S EVIDENCE REVIEWED

Time and tedium may both be economized by examining this testimony in chief of General Sherman, without waiting for his cross-examination by the defence. It must be recollected that the weight or point of the charge is, that the diary extracts, foreboding clanger and charging neglect and design in braving the danger without preparation—that these diary extracts were written after the foretold danger had occurred. If the specification is true, that is, writing the diary after the event, the charge is established; otherwise, the charge is not in accordance with the facts, or not true. If the statements of the diary are proven true, they cannot, in law, be taken as libelous, neither can they be taken as libelous or false, if it is proven they were written before the event, when they were mere conjectures, and by no means libels or falsities.

It may further be considered that all statements of the diary not pronounced and proven false by the prosecutor are to be taken as true. Proceeding on such data, the entry of March 26th, that an attack is indicated by the country people, and by the fact, not denied, that the rebel pickets are around and too near us, is admitted as true. The entry of March 27th, that the attack on our pickets by the rebel cavalry is an indication that they are covering some forward movement, is thus admitted by the pros-

---

1. If that only was the object of the expedition, why not remain at Savannah? Because then he could not have invited a battle so easily. This is one of the strongest points against these juggles.

ecutor as true, and so proven by the event. The entry of March 28th, that an attack on our camp would not be dangerous to an enemy under existing neglect or design, is also admitted as true, and so proven by the event.

Saturday, *March 29th.*—The refusal to allow the requisition for the axes is admitted, and an inference is plain, from the prosecutor's evidence, that there were axes to be had, which is contradicted by the evidence of the quartermaster and his sergeant, who both swear that no axes could be had till after the battle. He (Sherman) does not deny that an abattis (fallen trees) would prevent or avert an attack, except by stating on oath that defences would have invited an attack. "What a statement for any officer to make, and he a West Point Graduate. How insane, or idiotic, or what? for it can be nothing less than insanity, or idiocy which is worse, or a mere spiteful, childish, womanish denial, for the mere indulgence of contradiction—to say that an abattis would not have averted an attack which he had invited, which he does not deny.

Monday *March 31st.*—It is stated that, through the pickets, there are indications of attack. We having heard on good authority of many thousands of the enemy being five miles off, at Monterey, toward Corinth: and Captain Sharp, 46th Ohio, testifies that there were five thousand rebel troops at Monterey the 1st of April, 1862.

General Sherman testifies that this entry of the 31st of March must have been fabricated after its date, because our squadrons, regiments, and brigades were on the ground five days after it was made. Suppose they were on the ground, &c., as they were not—for he says that from the 31st of March to the 2nd of April part of his division was up at Eastport, and there is an inference that the charge of making the entry after its date was elicited by his (Sherman's) supposition that the writer intended to indicate this absence as a sure means of inviting an attack, as it was, while the entry, for other reasons, had been made before his return. Nor is it true that either "squadrons, regiments, and brigades" were on the ground (in our front) five days after the 31st of March. He says he was away the 1st, till the 2nd, late on which, and the 3rd, he had scouting parties out at night, which is one day, and perhaps a little more, of the five.

He was out on the 4th, in the afternoon, part of a day, and first tells of knowing there were the elements of an array in his front. This is two days of the five. He tells on this day, the 4th, that he did not know the destination and purpose of an enemy from whom there was reason to expect an attack the 3rd. On the 5th he says he had no cavalry. But to go back to the 31st of March, the main entry of which is, that Sherman is inviting an attack for which we are unprepared. This was not only the case, but the troops were purposely kept unprepared. All knew that the woods in front should have been cut away.

The colonel of the 46th had cleared off the woods and other obstacles in front and rear, and other regiments, seeing an Old Graduate preparing for danger, would have followed his example, on the right, at least, as they afterwards fortified on the march to Corinth. But axes could not be had on requisition, and there was not one grindstone in camp till two came up for the 46th Ohio on the 5th, late in the afternoon.[2] Quartermaster Giesy, of the 46th, testified that he never could get either clothing or tools before the battle.

The quartermaster sergeant, Parsons, testifies that he never could get even the twenty-two axes, a requisition for which was allowed, till after the battle, and that the division quartermaster would receive no stores turned over to him before the battle, the meaning of which is this:

> In the early, and indeed in all stages of the war, to save time and attention, &c., all sorts of stores, and especially tools, went anywhere or nowhere; one regiment would get the supply of three or four, and thus two or three were destitute until the over-supplied regiment turned the surplus over to some quartermaster, to be redistributed. But Sher-

---

2. Ordered by its colonel; the quartermaster keeping no such implements. (W. P. G.)

man would not allow his quartermaster to receive stores in this way, lest; he (Sherman) should be made responsible. This he said himself, as can easily be proven by at least one officer of volunteers, who remonstrated with him on the consequences at Pittsburgh. These consequences were, that there were no tools to fortify, and these stores were thrown away, unless turned over by one regimental quartermaster to another. In this way a few axes were got on the 5th of April by the 46th from the 57th, but it was too late. And in this way, by refusing even the means of defence, even ammunition, was dug the graves of the thousands who alone held their ground at Shiloh, and hold it yet; and this is justified on the ground that defences would have invited an attack.

In his evidence as to the entry of the 31st, Sherman upsets his whole charge of "fabrication," made the moment before by his own evidence, that for weeks Col. Worthington had been predicting the worst—that is predicting, he says, defeat for want of defences. It is not the fact that Colonel W. openly predicted defeat,[3] but he expected it, and with a really energetic enemy it would have occurred about the 1st of April, 1862, or ten days before that date, on the junction of Johnson with Bragg, at Corinth, the 20th March. The entry of April 3, that there was disorder at the landing, Sherman declares to be false and libelous, but swears there was confusion no general could have prevented. What's the difference between confusion and disorder? The entry of April 3rd suggests indications of an attack.

In the cross-examination he swears it is false that there were indications of an attack on the 3rd, because no stronger position was ever held by an army clearly a sequitur? though while he knew there was no hostile party within six miles on the 3rd, there was reason, he swears, to expect an attack.

Here he swears the same thing to be false and true. He says afterwards, on the 4th of April, there was no hostile party known

3. See McDowell's evidence.

before that day nearer than Monterey, which is but five miles out on the map which General Grant says was made by Colonel McPherson; and General Buell states Monterey at the same distance; and Captain Sharpe, the picket officer of the 46th, states this skirmish of the 4th at two and a half miles from camp, which is likely the distance, and not six miles. The diary entry of April 3rd states that the pickets are scarce a mile out, meaning, of course, those of the 46th Ohio. This Sherman also swears is false, and also swears that the Howell house, proven a main picket station of the 46th Ohio, was but three-fourths of a mile in front of his right centre brigade. (See cross-examination.)

The entry of April 3rd suggests that the troops cover too much ground (*i.e.*, the divisions are too far apart.) This General Sherman swears is false, and testifies that we did not occupy too much ground. "General Buell's forces had been expected rightfully for two weeks, and a place or gap was left for his forces, though General Grant afterward had determined to send Buell to Hamburgh," (four miles above.)

Here again is evidence, pitched up and knocked down, as are infidels in the Mohammedan "inferno." Monkir pitches them up on a red-hot fork, and Nekir knocks them back with a white-hot sledge to all eternity, or sufficiently purified for true believers. The military term "occupying two much ground," means that there are gaps in a line of troops. Sherman swears that that gap is no gap, if intended to be filled; that the intention of filling it has been altered; and he swears in terms that the intention to fill the gap with troops intended for another post makes a falsehood of the suggestion that there was any gap to be filled in the line.

So it was left open over a mile wide for the enemy, by which to attack our flanks and rear, as he says in his report the enemy did to some purpose on the 6th of April, 1862. Having thus answered its intended purpose of letting in the enemy, without making use of Buell's troops, either to fill the gap at Shiloh or fall on the rebel right and rear at Hamburgh, he closes the gap on the plan of the battle, which Badeau says was drawn by

McPherson and corrected by both Grant and Sherman. These being all West Pointers, who dare deny the perfection of the map made since the battle? to back up Sherman's evidence. To fill this gap on the improved and corrected and certified battle plan of Shiloh. Prentiss is allowed an additional brigade he had not in the battle, and McClernand has very kindly furnished the flank of a brigade to fill up that line for which the imaginary brigade of Prentiss was insufficient. So, on the map corrected since the appropriate use of the same gap by the enemy on the 6th, we find a front respectably patched up for future history, to accompany Sherman's equally truthful letter of January, 1865, for future history, as he says.

But, badinage thus provoked aside, how long will it be that such evidence proves even a West Point Graduate fitted to command all the armies of the Union, with nothing better to prove his capacity? It may also as well be repeated here, as will be seen by battle plan No. 2, that Sherman's reported position of the three front divisions, if true, entirely upsets this patched-up arrangement, and, with flanks to the front, leaves a gap of two miles, where there was really but one mile before, and this arrangement is not much, if any, worse than that which existed with regard to these divisions at 7 a. m. on the 6th of April, 1862. But to return to the present commander-in-chief, as to his generalship and vigilance two days before the advent of that battle, on which really rest his position and reputation as a great military strategist and tactician, such as was wanted by the Washington ring for the sole purpose of spinning out the war.

The diary of April 3rd further suggests, that the scattered condition of the troops, (denied by General Sherman, see map 2, with flanks to the front,) in case of a sudden attack, might drive them back in detail all of which occurred, according to the diary, as is generally admitted, and among others by General Sherman himself in his report and by his admirers. The diary of Friday, the 4th, barely refers to the picket affair of that afternoon. The brigade orders to stack arms were suggested by Colonel W. to Colonel McDowell. The negligence charged refers to the destitution of tools and defences, the failure to close up the gaps and make roads in rear of the lines, to cut away the timber and brush in front, and make some preparation for the imminent attack.

In his evidence, as to the entries of April 3rd, is a digression by General Sherman, which this narrator is compelled to follow, as it refers to the choice of the ground on which the battle was fought. No one had imputed the choice of this ground to General Grant, though it is plain it had his approval before it was occupied by the Union army. Bowman says that on the 14th March General Sherman, with the leading division of Grant's army, passed up the Tennessee; so of course he was under the orders of General Grant, who the day before (the 13th) had been "relieved from his disgrace," &c., and reached Pittsburgh the 17th. Orders were first given by Sherman to unload the boats of the camp equipage the 18th, and the camp was not really established till next day, 19th. Bowman, indorsed by Sherman, further says, that Halleck decided to advance up the Tennessee river as far as practicable by water, then to debark on the west bank, &c., &c.

Grant is then plainly responsible for the debarkation at Pittsburgh landing, and doubtless had Halleck's authority to land on the west side. No objection to Bowman's statement was ever made by either Grant or Halleck, and there is ample ground for Whitelaw Reed's statement that men of rank and ability have denied that the choice of this camp can be laid on General C. F. Smith, as charged by Sherman in the course of this evidence, when it was irrelevant and uncalled-for: thus proving the choice his own.

Smith was a prudent soldier, when in a healthy state of mind and body; which he was not, entirely, after the capture of Fort Donelson.

It is a slander on his memory, of which Sherman affects to be so careful, to say that he ever approved of such an expedition as that to Eastport, under such circumstances, when the roads were impassable and flooded, and when Grant supposed not less than 40,000 of the enemy were along the railroad between Decatur and Corinth, as was the fact; when Badeau considered Grant's situation at Pittsburgh in imminent need of Buell's force of 40,000 men, and Grant, aware of the danger, "had not been at Savannah one hour, on the 17th, when he sent up Smith and McClernand as fast as boats could carry them."

On the 14th he (Sherman) was under command of Grant, acting under orders of Halleck, to establish a camp on the west side of the river. Sherman went up, then, on the 14th, he says, under Grant's orders, and came down to Pittsburgh on the 16th, under Smith's orders, as he swears Monkir and Nekir again. On the 18th he issues the first orders to go into camp at Shiloh, Grant then being at Savannah, but Smith again in command, if Sherman is worthy of credit on his own contradictory evidence, which less credulous people than this commentator might doubt, if he were not commander-in-chief, &c., at present.

Sherman says he had orders from General Smith, and took post accordingly. Took post on the 18th and 19th, under Smith's command, when Grant was himself at Savannah, on the 17th, ordering Smith up, as Badeau says, and says in terms, that he and Grant, as to the history of Grant, are responsible for each other, as to the facts. "*Par nobile fratrum!*" Yet Sherman says Smith's own division took post, under Smith's orders, thus contradicting Grant and Badeau. What ought such evidence to be worth from any one except a commander-in-chief, or the President himself, as to who located camp Shiloh? And then, after this endeavor to shift the responsibility, as to the choice of the camp, from himself and Grant to C. F. Smith, he proceeds in the most nonsensically extravagant laudation of the location:

"Even as we were, (without defences,) on the 6th of April, the world afforded no more advantageous field of battle."

For the purposes intended was doubtless a mental reservation for which he very likely had antecedent, as he did have subsequent absolution, and a very substantial blessing and testimonial from Halleck. Though this matter must be repeated, yet to maintain the thread of this digest of indigestive evidence, it may or must come in here.

"Flanks well protected," says the commander-in-chief, "and never threatened; troops in easy support; timber and broken ground giving good points to rally," &c. Now, if we are to believe his division report of April 10, 1862, the flanks, in many cases, were turned merely by a threatened advance of the enemy, and the protection of the creeks was nothing, not even equal to the twig that abraded the back of his bridle hand, to the extent of a half dime of surface, and passed for a ball through it. Troops in easy support, he says, when no separate divisions were nearer than four hundred to eighteen hundred yards, with interposing woods or hollows. Timber and broken ground, which enabled the enemy to approach within half musket-shot of his front, and was far more advantageous to an advancing foe than to a retreating force, which it was distinctly understood he calculated and expected the force under his command would and perhaps was intended to be. So says Whitelaw Reed.

And he proceeds to prove the advantages of this field, by stating that, in consequence of the strength of the position, but 10,000 or more of the troops who held their ground ran away, while the main body was not driven back farther than two and a half to eleven miles, or from Shiloh to Snake creek and Savannah. Against these 60,000 chosen troops of the South there were some 3,000 of the Union soldiers, who alone held their ground, and hold it yet. They died, the price of that blood-stained ground, for the possession of which no soldier on either side need to have lost a drop of blood, had Buell's troops, on Saturday afternoon, been sent, as intended, to Hamburgh, four miles above.

Who for this shall, in the future, be held responsible Halleck, or Grant, or Sherman; or those who, to prolong the war for political purposes, made the sacrifice necessary, as Sherman says not only for the purpose he avows,[4] but for the promotion and emolument of

---

4. It was necessary that a combat, fierce and bitter, should come off, to test the manhood of the two armies: that is, for the mere purpose of a battle, (as this writer charged at the time,) to get him promoted.

those who upheld this horrid policy at the capital and in the field?

But to return to the evidence: "On Friday, the 4th," says General Sherman, "no officer nor soldier, not even Colonel Worthington, looked for an attack, as I can prove."

"Grant had marched twelve miles," Badeau says, "from Fort Henry to Fort Donelson, in half a day."

The distance from Shiloh Church to Corinth is about sixteen miles, and the distance from Hamburgh to Corinth, being about the same, was marched by the 81st Ohio in seven hours, during the winter of 1863; hence the danger of so close an enemy.

It has been be shown, also, that General Sherman believed this very day that the enemy was in sufficient force in his immediate front to justify them in an attack and justify him in expecting one, this 4th of April, 1862. Soon after noon he says he heard distant musketry, and finally three cannon shot, which could not be ours.

This was the first positive information of any approaching force—nearer than Monterey, (five miles.) He at once rode out one and a half miles, and there waited the return of Colonel Buckland and Major Ricker, who reported encountering infantry, artillery, and cavalry. "We then knew," says Sherman, "we had the elements of an army in our front, but did not know its strength or destination" or destination! Here is a major general who has testified that there was reason to expect an attack on the 3rd of April, the day before—who has had reason to believe the enemy had over 60,000 men at or near Corinth; who knew, or thought he knew, the rebel army had marched from Corinth on the morning of the day before, (the 3rd;)—and he here makes oath that there was no reason to expect an attack after twenty-four hours had elapsed since the actual or supposed march from Corinth had begun! If he did believe in this absence of danger, was he fit for a commander? And if, in the presence of such danger, he, on the morning of the 5th, removed his cavalry and artillery from his front to the rear, as he did remove them, is he an idiot, or worse?

But he repeats this assumption of ignorance. He had to guess the purpose of this enemy in his front, who had announced himself by the discharge of artillery and musketry. He sees wolf-tracks about a sheep-fold, or a hawk hovering over a chicken yard, and has to guess alike the purpose of the wolf or hawk, or enemy lying before him. But this is no worse than swearing that there was no gap in a line, because it was to have been filled by Buell, who was to have been sent up to Hamburgh. He then adds, with the utmost self-gratulation and self-approval, that no general could have detected the approach of an enemy sooner than he had done by allowing that enemy to approach unmolested within gun-shot of his camp.

After such testifying as this, it is superfluous to say anything about his statement, in terms, that he had, on the 3rd of April, gone through and one mile beyond Monterey,[5] on the road to Corinth, where there had been 5,000 or more of the enemy for near a week before. He tells us, through Bowman, that the importance of the crisis was apparent, and that Buell was tardy in his march towards Shiloh, knowing the danger threatening the Army of the Tennessee, as Badeau says, on and after the 17th March. Or that seventeen days before this time (the 4th of April, 1862) there was danger, and yet Sherman swears, on the 4th, there was none, and proves it as above.

"Thus, while Buckland," he continues, "was guarding safely our front, the colonel of another brigade, in a safe corner, was looking for an attack every hour," thus again upsetting his charge of fabricating apprehension of an attack, after the event had passed. This witness then proceeds to say that Colonel W. could have heard of no such thing as rebel artillery across the valley from the camp; and this same evidence is thrice repeated in the course of his examination. He states that he has given a history of events during a week preceding the battle—"From the 2nd to the 7th of April I have given an account."

What account has he given of anything occurring Friday night, or Saturday, or Saturday night, or Sunday, or Sunday

---

5. If he went out, as he says, six miles, he must have gone a mile beyond Monterey, according to his official map. W. P. G.

night? Not a word. As will be seen, he denies everything material which occurred, and which plainly, as the lightning foretells the thunder, foretold the bloody storm of death and destruction Grant and he had invoked, and which was hovering over that beguiled and fated army. The storm, which he of course avoided doing anything to avert, and of which, for his own personal purposes, was the veriest demon, from the fatal whirr of its first deadly shaft, till it had strewn its myriads of murdered and mangled victims over its crimsoned track; all of this slaughter and destruction inuring to the benefit of those who were and now are their blood-stained architects, whether in or out of the Army of the Tennessee in the West, or the political war "ring" at Washington.

Note. The most fallacious part of the statement by Sherman, as to what occurred during the week before the battle, is that, in which he swears that our squadrons, regiments, and brigades were on the ground (in front, of course) five days after the 31st of March, 1862. He then swears, as noted, that from the 31st to the 2nd he was at Eastport; and he also swears on cross-examination that he had no cavalry at his command on the 5th of April, the very day before the battle. He says not a word of what is made known by Colonel Stuart and Lieutenant Fitch, that the artillery was also withdrawn on the morning of the 5th. He is silent about the pickets being driven in and the rebel artillery in his front the same day. And in this state of facts he swears that, knowing a hostile army to be in front, which there is evidence he believed had 60,000 men, he did not know their destination and had to guess their purpose.

He had then no squadrons, regiments, or brigades out on the 5th, and his five days are thus, by his own showing, reduced to two, on neither of which was he ever three miles beyond the front of his camp. Could Argus, of the hundred eyes, have been more vigilant? But his five days of activity, stated as such, are on oath reduced to little over two; and yet again, on oath, these two are at the close of his evidence increased to seven, like Falstaff's men in buckram, to which are gratuitously added three days after the battle in going up to destroy the Bear-creek bridge.

This point, being at the time undefended, passes among his deeds of chivalry into the same category as the heroic action related by the venerable philosopher, such as the valiant destruction of a very dangerous but abandoned rebel camp and the more glorious capture of a hospital empty, or filled with sick and wounded men our modern Franklin does not say. Such an omission!

Chapter 10

Sherman's Cross-Examination and the Counter Evidence Against Him

I was perfectly willing that the enemy should attack us and think Beauregard made a fatal mistake when he did it; but I deny that the enemy had a battery near the Howell house that afternoon, April 5, 1862. (Sherman's cross-examination August, 1862.)

Captain Sharpe, 46th Ohio, was sworn and testifies:

I saw the piece of artillery myself to the right of the Widow Howell's house. I reported the circumstance to General Sherman, who said he would have the (his) artillery in readiness. (Record of Colonel Washington's trial at Memphis, August, 1862.)

General Sherman, being asked what entries of the 3rd of April were false in this diary, replied, as above stated, that it was false to state that Sherman had forbidden his quartermaster receiving anything, (stores;) that there were indications of an attack, is false; that we covered too much ground, is false; that our pickets were only a mile out, is false, &c.; and on question as to whether he heard of any rebel artillery near the Howell house Saturday afternoon, he answered that he had not. He testifies that on Saturday, the 5th, he had no cavalry subject to his orders, but about dark that evening eight companies of the 4th Illinois reported to him for duty.

He testified "that no pickets were driven out of the Howell

house on Saturday. The house," he says, "which I call the Widow Howell's house, was in a field, near a lane, in Buckland's front, about three-quarters of a mile from his centre. Our pickets were a mile in front of that house. I was perfectly willing the enemy should attack us, and think Beauregard made a fatal mistake when he did it; but I deny that the enemy had a battery near the Howell house that Saturday afternoon.

The house was in a large field, and no place for pickets. It was not a picket station, and pickets there were of no use. The fork of the road in front was the key-point of the attack, and that point was watched.

"Did you know," asked Colonel W., "that the pickets were driven in from Weaver's house on Saturday?"

"Answer. I know of no such house; no such house was a picket station. None of the pickets were driven in" (on Saturday, April 5th.)

"I know," said the prosecutor, at the close of his cross-examination, "that Colonel Worthington knew his duties well, and wondered that he should disregard them."

On question by Colonel Worthington, whether he, to Sherman's knowledge, had ever neglected any duty in his regiment, Sherman answered, "I will allege none except such as are charged here; I leave that to his brigadier."

The evidence above given will show what ground there was for the charge of conduct unworthy of an officer and a gentleman, and for the specification that he had fabricated a false diary after the event, (the battle,) and this, when none but an idiot would fabricate or write anything but the facts that really occurred after their occurrence.

On being called again by the defence, General Sherman testified as follows:

The charges were substantially drawn by me. I placed the subject-matter in the hands of the judge advocate for trial. I heard nothing of any (rebel) guns on our left (front) on Saturday. I do not know Captain Sharpe; I may have seen him; I did not tell any person on Saturday afternoon that

I would have the artillery harnessed up, unless for inspection. (His artillery had been withdrawn.)

Rebel Artillery on the 5th

Colonel Buckland, (a great friend of General Sherman,) testifies:

All I heard of artillery on Saturday was this: Some of my pickets thought they had seen the glimmer of a brass gun. I looked, but could see nothing of the kind. I went over to General Sherman's headquarters and reported that some of the pickets thought they had seen artillery, but that I could not discover any.

Captain Sharpe, of the 46th Ohio, testified that

there was a piece of artillery near the Howell house, to the right, on Saturday evening. He supposed it was rebel artillery. It was pointed to our camp. It was first observed in the early part of the afternoon. I did not see it until 5 p. m. I reported the circumstance both to Colonel McDowell and General Sherman. General Sherman said he would have the (his) artillery in readiness. I saw the piece of artillery myself to the right of Widow Howell's house.

Lieutenant Crary, picket officer of the 46th Ohio, testified as to the artillery as follows:

Saturday afternoon, April 5th, I rode along the pickets of the 40th Illinois. They reported that they had seen several pieces of artillery posted near the Howell house, southeast of the house. I may have reported the number of guns at three, but I do not recollect doing so. I heard of some artillery that afternoon opposite Hildebrand's brigade, (the left.) I reported to Captain Harlan, on Colonel McDowell's staff.

Lieutenant Colonel C. C. Walcut, 46th Ohio, testified as follows:

I do not remember hearing of any artillery on Saturday,

April 5, except Captain Sharpe thought there was some. When leaving Paducah there was nothing but corn for the mules. We had but little ammunition.

Lieutenant Colonel (now Major General) Walcut was a particular friend and admirer of his patron, General Sherman. (W. P. G.)

EVIDENCE AS TO PICKETS OF SHERMAN'S DIVISION AT SHILOH, SATURDAY, April 5, 1862.

Colonel Buckland, commanding the 4th brigade, testifies:

"The pickets fell back Saturday morning without my orders."

(Much of Buckland's testimony has been eliminated from the record, and it was unwillingly given, unless in favour of Sherman.)

Colonel Hildebrand, commanding 3rd brigade, testifies:

The infantry pickets were driven in on Saturday. I endeavoured to replace them, but was prevented by the rebel cavalry. This was near Lee's house. Pickets were driven from that position some time in the afternoon of Saturday, the 5th April.

Captain Sharpe, chief picket officer of 46th Ohio volunteer infantry:

I went out on picket duty about the 25th March. Before Shiloh I made headquarters at Weaver's. About the 1st of April made a post at Widow Howell's. From Mrs. Howell's to Weaver's is three hundred or four hundred yards. Moore's is not more than half a mile from camp. There were two pickets fired on at Moore's March 25th to 27th by two cavalry. I was at a picket skirmish Friday evening, the 4th of April, about two and a half miles from camp. The pickets were driven from the Howell house on Saturday about 7 a. m.

There were no pickets that I know of in front of the

Howell house on the Corinth road. I never saw Colonel McDowell at picket there while I was there. I never saw General Sherman there. I was at Pea Ridge (5 miles) about April 1st. Drove in their pickets, and was informed by farmers that there were 5,000 infantry there. The pickets of McDowell's brigade on Saturday were at Moore's, (half mile from camp.) Howell's was recognized as one oif the picket posts of the 1st brigade, 5th division. The Howell house was on the left of our brigade. There were no pickets between my post and the enemy. I reported to Colonel McDowell habitually. I do not know of any pickets from any of the other brigades in front of the Howell house on Saturday, the day before the battle.

Question by Colonel W. 'Were not the enemy in possession of the Howell house all day Saturday?'

Answer. 'They were.'

Captain H. E. Giesy, company F, appeared, and was sworn.

Question by prisoner. 'Do you recollect my order for two companies to lie on their arms?'

Answer. 'I recollect your ordering two companies to lie on their arms the Friday before the battle. We had been drilling two weeks in the manual of arms, and you directed them to practice in loading and firing.'

Question by prisoner. 'Where did you first see the charges now under investigation?'

(Ruled out by the court as improper and irrelevant. Captain Giesy was the officer who obtained surreptitious possession of a proof sheet of Colonel W's diary extracts, and took the same to General Sherman, for which he was promoted to the majority of the regiment over seven or eight older in rank and abler captains.)

Colonel J. A. McDowell, commanding the brigade, testified as follows, on question by Colonel W.:

I do not know that I ever heard you predict any actual disaster. On Monday or Tuesday before the battle you insisted that we would be attacked, and complained of the want of tools.

Lieutenant George F. Crary, 46th Ohio, sworn:

Question by prisoner. 'Did you see me on Saturday morning out with the pickets?'
A. 'I saw you out there early in the morning. We were driven away about 7 a. m.,' (Sept. 5, 1862.) 'I heard a rebel drum beat Friday afternoon. The beat appeared to be in more than one regiment.'

Colonel David Stuart, 55th Illinois, testified:

Had no artillery on that day, (day of the battle.) It was taken away Saturday morning, and annexed to General Smith's division. If the artillery had remained, I think I should have lost it, from circumstances that occurred during the battle.

Timothy N. Ward, hospital steward, sworn, testified:

That while at Fort Pickering Colonel Worthington had visited the hospital almost daily. He had generally visited the hospital regularly on the march.

Colonel T. Kilby Smith, 54th Ohio, sworn, testified:

That his camp, in Sherman's 2nd brigade, was about three-quarters of a mile from and west of the river. When Lick Creek was fordable at the Hamburgh Ford, it was fordable above, (*everywhere.*)

(*Much of an omission here. W. P. G.*)
Testified further:

That, when shown the diary extracts, he was told that they were to be considered confidential. That Colonel W. had told him at the time that he had written or intended to write a letter to go to him (Halleck) with the diary extracts.

Lieutenant J. A. Fitch, Waterhouse's battery, sworn:

On the evening of April 5, the battery was near Sherman's headquarters, about sixty *rods* from (and in rear of) Shiloh Church. Barrett's battery was on our left. The park faced to the river. Came into camp on the 5th April, (at dark.)

(*This puts the flank of the artillery to the front. W. P. G.*)

It will be seen by Colonel Smith's evidence that there was no use for the 2nd brigade where it was. Watching the ford was all a pretence; and Lick Creek, as a defence, was utterly worthless, being fordable all the way up when fordable at the Hamburgh crossing.

Lieutenant Fitch swears that the artillery was not parked in line of battle, as Sherman says it was in his report. He also testified that he came in at the same time as the 4th Illinois Cavalry—about dark. (*Record mutilated, as in many other cases.*)

OBSERVATIONS ON THE TESTIMONY OF THE DEFENCE.

It is plain that, as to the fabrication of the diary after the event, the point of the charge and specifications of conduct unbecoming an officer and a gentleman, Sherman has settled the matter by his evidence against the truth of the charge and specification. The question then arises, what is the mental constitution of any man who repeatedly and deliberately convicts himself of every charge against himself in the diary, on which he founds the charge of falsehood and libel?

Swearing it is false, and admitting on oath that it is true in most cases, and swearing against notorious facts as to the pickets and rebel artillery, plainly because he had failed to mention them in his report, and failing to mention them, because such mention would be evidence of more than the neglect charged by the diary itself—Is such a man of sound and or substantive integrity, or not? Eminent lawyers are of opinion that this evidence against plain facts cannot properly be considered perjury, because the statements are so easily overturned outside his own evidence, if that were not sufficient.

Calling these statements, then, the mere ebullitions of ill temper or unguardedness, or vindictiveness, they demonstrate at least one thing; that is, the perfect confidence of impunity, confidence in association or league with these, or toleration or license from those for whose benefit or whose objects these reckless actions or contradictory or anomalous statements are made; and the same reckless confidence, not only of impunity, but of official approbation, runs through all this commander's words and operations, down to the Jo. Johnston treaty at Durham station, where the object of his employment for the protraction of the war having ceased, it became necessary to check a career which, if permitted further, might have exposed all the nefarious jobbing, juggling, and selfish, intriguing policy of the political cabal at Washington throughout the war.

On the theory of his employment for such a purpose, and on no other, can his unaccountable and extravagant words and actions become intelligible. His outrageous order of March, 1867, attaching all the great military bureaus to his personal staff, and his bullying letter to Congress as to his pay, are all traceable to the same source, and require to be curbed in time, by putting him out of a place he is unfit for. And now to a brief exposition of the balance of the evidence brought out on this cross-examination, for the purpose of obtaining which this trial was striven for with rather too much success, according to the result, by the prisoner in the case.

The truth of all the diary extracts, charged by the prosecutor as false, having been proven, such extracts require little more attention. The withdrawal of the cavalry pickets on Saturday morning, when plainly more necessary than before, was so extraordinary an incident, that General Sherman, after swearing that his squadrons of cavalry, &c., were in the front from the 1st to the 6th of April, expunges his veracity, as usual, by the evidence that he had no cavalry subject to his command on Saturday, the 5th of April, 1862.

From Senator Sherman's speech in the Congressional Globe of May, 1862, it will be seen that this same withdrawal of his cavalry pickets has been stated in a letter to his brother, the Senator, thus making Grant clearly responsible for a measure calculated to induce an attack; to prevent, by the capture of a picket, any news reaching the enemy of Buell's vicinity, and doubtless intended to lull the Union army into security, when on the verge of destruction. The driving back of the pickets of three brigades is clearly proven by Buckland, Hildebrand, and officers Sharp and Crary. It is plainly proven that all day of the 5th, after 7 a. m., the Howell house, a most important picket station, three-fourths of a mile from Sherman's centre, was in possession of the enemy.

His persistent swearing that no rebel artillery was or could possibly have been seen or heard of in his front that day (the 5th) is clear proof, if any were wanting of his entire knowledge of the fact proven by his especial friends, Buckland and Walcot, and picket officers Crary and Sharpe, 46th Ohio. Not a word of what this evidence disclosed was dispatched to Halleck, (who did not want it,) nor to the War Office at Washington, as required by article 34 of the Army Regulations; nor was such news wanted there, and if there, it would have been, long ere this, removed or destroyed.

This evidence was examined at the Judge Advocate General's office. This false swearing could not have been unnoticed. What is then the inference? What else than that this promoter or rectifier of justice was also in the interest of the combined cabals in and out of Congress, in the Cabinet, or in the field? And here it may be mentioned that, as part of the plan to prolong the war without making the policy public, article 34, section 448 (perhaps) of the Army Regulations, requiring the commanders of armies in the field, generals of divisions, &c., to forward from day to day their orders issued, and important information obtained, was dispensed with in this campaign, especially in the case of General Sherman, and, of course, that of other officers in the war.

(Sherman swears he was perfectly willing the enemy should attack us, and thinks Beauregard made a fatal mistake when he did it. He thus proves the truth of the diary entry of March 31st, that he was inviting an attack for which we were not prepared, which he has denied, yet, in

contradiction,as usual, he tells Colonel Buckland reprovingly, that on the 4th he might have brought on an attack, for which we were not ready on that day. He was, of course, less prepared on the 5th, when the cavalry and artillery were withdrawn. And on the 6th, with no axes before that day to clear off and defend the front, we were not prepared for anything but the defeat that followed. So, while expecting an attack [it cannot be too often repeated] on the 3rd and on the 4th, and more than ever defenceless, with an enemy in gunshot, on the 5th he writes to Grant he has no expectation of an attack. And knowing all the incidents of Saturday, Grant dispatches an order to Halleck, "Not the least danger, but will be prepared if there is" for a defeat. W. P. G.)

Sherman swears that he was willing that the enemy should make the attack, but made a fatal mistake in making it. Here is a plain expression of his mental reservation, that, as he knew, the attack would have been fatal to the enemy if Buell's troops had been sent up to Hamburgh at any time before daylight, or even later, on the 6th, to fall upon the rebel right and rear, in camp little if any thing over a mile, by Grant's and Badeau's map, from that place.

All this Sherman tells us should have been done when he says the attack was a mistake, which, instead of being fatal to Beauregard, was fatal to 13,000 Union troops. What else could have made the rebel attack fatal to them but the exposure of their right and rear, which would have been fatal if Buell had been sent up as intended. It is one of the most unaccountable events of the war that A. S. Johnson should have occupied such a dangerous position a single moment. The only reason which can be given that it was not fatal to his army is, that Grant and Sherman, acting by authority, designed and preferred the slaughter and loss of 13,000 Union troops to a total defeat of the enemy, in which Buell's troops should have had a part, or preferred a defeat, because essential to prolong the war, as this defeat did prolong it.

Beauregard himself, as has been written, was aware of the danger of an attack where he was Saturday afternoon, and a single messenger from Grant Saturday afternoon or night, with news that Nelson's division was at Savannah, would have scattered the hostile army like autumn leaves. Grant knew, and it is believed was urged to attack by McPherson, who knew, from a reconnaissance, that the enemy were at the bend of Lick creek, north-west of Hamburgh.

Sherman closes this remarkable and almost unconscious disclosure of his intentional neglect or failure to send up Buell's troops, by the repeated denial, on oath, that there was hostile artillery Saturday afternoon near the Howell house. And he swears this, while he knew that the enemy had more than one battery two or three miles out the day before, with nothing to prevent them taking possession of our picket stations next day, as they did. This evidence against plain facts is clearly to cover the criminal withdrawal of his own artillery, to show the enemy that he had no suspicion of their immediate presence; a presence made known by their cannon and musketry the day before, as well as by Major Ricker's assurance that he had met the van of Beauregard's army on the 4th in the afternoon. This is another phase of Shermanic strategy.

He then proceeds, in his usual absurd and self-contradictory way, to swear that there were no pickets at the Ho well house, or, if there, were of no use there. That, nevertheless, the key -point towards his centre was the fork of the road in front of the house, and that that point was watched; yet he says in the same breath it was no place for pickets. How was it watched except by pickets or guards, or sentinels, supposed to be out of sight of the camp? He was right in his statement that the road fork near the house was a key-point, where hostile marching columns could unite for the attack on his centre, as they did next morning. The first rebel troops seen by this narrator on Sunday morning were marching past the Howell house.

That was the reason, (the direct road to our centre passed this point) why it had been held by the hostile artillery the day before. Here is where part of Sherman's artillery should have been, instead of in his rear, and this is one key of his perpetual denial of artillery at a point . which proclaimed Grant's criminal neglect and his own; or, if this was the result of design, the design made them the mere hired instruments of party operators in patronage and blood.

Then, as if to clinch the flimsy fabric of his evidence with a handful of sand, he swears wildly that no Union pickets were driven in on Saturday, the day before the battle. This was sworn in the face of the direct evidence of his whole division, had it been called up, and the question again arises, what could have given him confidence in impunity and approbation, except the contract and collusion established by his every act as a commander, and every word as a witness against an officer he had commended for his conduct on the field; an officer who had striven hard without avail, against his opposition, to rescue that army from the bloody and disastrous fate for which, by him and Grant, it had purposely been prepared.

General Grant, as has been related, was out at Shiloh Saturday afternoon, and remained on his boat at the landing till near 11 p. m. of that day, the 5th. If it has not been recorded, it may have reference here that Grant, in his history by Badeau, barely mentions that he rode out to Sherman's lines the day after the 4th, and concurred with him that there was no danger of an attack both had expected, according to Sherman's evidence, on the 3rd and 4th previous. But to conceal that this was the 5th, he states immediately after, that in returning from the front on the 4th Grant was hurt by a fall from his horse. It is however distinctly to be understood from Badeau that on the 5th, after giving an, order to Nelson, Grant having made all his preparations for removing his headquarters to Pittsburgh on the morrow, did not go out to Shiloh, but remained to meet Buell, as that officer had desired, Buell having, by dispatch on the 4th, desired to meet him at Savannah on the 5th.

Now, with such plain subterfuge, planned with so much secretive care, plain to any narrator seeking for truth, what respect or indulgence can the author of such petty deception merit, whatever his position, and supposing his service as a commander had been anything but worse than negative in its character. Especially when, upon such subterfuge, ignorance is feigned of the occurrences of April 5th, when, with all these occurrences before him, he dispatches to Halleck that day or night that he has not the faintest idea of an attack he evidently has been expecting for at least three days before. He knew everything about the driving in of the pickets on the 5th, and the presence of rebel artillery in sight through the woods, from the Union picket posts within a few hundred yards of the camp. Sherman testifies on oath, and writes to his brother, the Senator, that Grant had taken away his cavalry pickets early Saturday morning, and this is confirmed by Major Ricker, 5th Ohio cavalry. Grant knew also that, as Captain Stuart swears, the artillery of Sherman's line had, the same morning, been taken to the rear, and Stuart's was not returned at all.

All this had been done on the morning of the 5th, with the knowledge that on the 4th, as Sherman swears, he knew there were the elements of a hostile army in his front, when their drum beats had been heard, yet these " great commanders were innocent of the destination and purpose of this army," so welcomed by them to their open front and unsuspecting troops. The cannon and musketry with which Sherman says they announced their presence on the 4th appears and remains at our picket posts all next day to take a regular rest and brush up for attack, and yet a dispatch goes to headquarters that as Sherman says all is quiet along my lines, and Grant repeats, "All's well," as it was for the protraction of the war by the destruction of a Union army of 40,000 men. And then, because of the place and power thus attained, it is gravely argued that these commanders must be treated with all the respect and consideration purchased by crimes like these. If there is any other explanation, let it be made known.

Now, to sum this matter up again with truth, and not with fiction, or silence, or concealment, as has been always done, what is the condition of affairs on Saturday night, the 5th of April, 1862, under which the commander at the camp writes to the commander at Savannah that "he does not apprehend an attack on his position?"

By his own evidence, well sustained in this case, Sherman had reason to expect an attack on his position on the 3rd of April. He admitted to Buckland apprehension of an attack on the 4th of April, on which day Nelson is informed that he is not wanted till the 8th. The enemy drive in his pickets, and occupy his nearest picket station with their cannon on the 5th, on which day he not only sends no cavalry pickets out, but his cavalry and artillery are withdrawn to the rear. All such active and energetic preparations to meet the enemy are made on the eve of battle, in accordance with the Grant-Shermanic strategy and tactics of keeping all flanks presented to the enemy,, and avoiding defences, which invite an attack.

These are the preparations in accordance with the dictates of the protractive policy. Grant knows on the day of these organizations for defeat, *i.e.* on the 5th, that Nelson's division of say 7,000 men is at Savannah before noon of that day, spite of advice to keep back and not intrude on his and Sherman's battleground till wanted. And this intrusion is the more impertinent, since Grant and Sherman knew Saturday afternoon that the right flank and rear of the adventurous Southrons is little over a mile (by Badeau) from the Tennessee river at Hamburgh, two miles above our left at Shiloh. Grant knows that by a movement of our army that night, or in early morning, a few miles out on the lower Purdy and west Corinth roads, his troops will be in position to attack the rebel left.

He knows that the divisions of Lew. Wallace at Crump's, and Nelson with Buell at Savannah, can run up to Hamburgh at any appointed hour of the night of the 5th, or early morning of the 6th of April, 1862, when there will be say 14,000 Union troops on the rebel right and rear, and near 40,000 opposite their left and centre. And he knows that by such simple dispositions of the Union troops the hostile army must be scattered or captured without material bloodshed.

And now, was it because of his unwillingness that Buell's troops should have a share in such success, or because of secret instructions, under agreement to prolong the war, by the loss of a battle, that he foregoes all this easy advantage, and allows our army to sleep in false security? Does he, for the furtherance of this "protraction," hide from his own and from Buell' s troops the presence of the enemy, leaving them thus exposed to wanton slaughter, and sacrifices 13,000 Union soldiers to his own blind and bloody jealousy, or for the political purposes of the Washington cabal, let his preparations for disaster reach their legitimate or illegitimate result.

If his reasons were personal, what, in comparison to this, was the whole crime of the rebellion, and why should he so long have enjoyed power and impunity instead of punishment? If under instructions or by agreement, what punishment would be too severe for both principals and instruments of such atrocity? If it was mere stupidity, stolidity, or incapacity, what should be the fate of his employers, and why should he remain in power where he is? Whatever the private motive—whatever the party or public policy—the salient result is plain and prominent. A glorious and next to bloodless victory was given up to the enemy—worse than thrown away—on the 6th; exchanged for intended disaster by the Union commander; bartered for future place and patronage by the Washington cabal; and 40,000 Union troops sold, labelled, and consigned to a bloody and disgraceful defeat.

Who can, on the evidence of the above-stated trial, with collateral incidents and facts, put any other construction on the acts and neglects of these commanders before, on, and after the 6th day of April. 1862.

The great effort of Grant and Badeau, Sherman and Bowman, has been to impress upon the public, as they seem to have done successfully, that if Buell had been up in time, not only would the disaster of the 6th have been prevented, but they would have attacked the Confederate army. Buell was up in time, and the most favourable time for the utter rout of the enemy, yet they made no use of these troops, when, as all admit and none deny, an attack would have been a victory. This refusal, then, of these

Army of the Ohio troops, when they were upon time, and exact time, is ample evidence of keeping Buell back, even if that of General Ammen and Grant's dispatch to Nelson, of April 4th, were wanting. And for this "tardiness" Buell has been branded with disloyalty, and, to prove it, the record of his inquiry court, proving the criminality of his accusers, has by them been made away with. The two salient points, then, to prove the protractive war policy upon the administration of 1862, are, first, the placing of Buell, who was for the capture of the upper Tennessee, under Halleck, who prevented it; and, second, the keeping back of Buell from the field of Shiloh, and eventually driving him from the army, and the advancement of Grant, not only for keeping him back, but for refusing his troops, when they came up in time to defeat the enemy, April 5, 1862.

The diary extracts, on which is founded this commentary, and on which it was endeavoured to establish a charge of unmilitary and ungentlemanly conduct against its writer—these diary extracts were written ten years ago to fulfil their present mission, as is witnessed by one of the aids of Sherman, under whose charge the 1st brigade of his division was devoted to the "infernal gods." This was in substitution for himself in a very anti Roman Decius style; but the evidence of the intention above stated is as follows from the record: Major W. D. Sanger, aid to General Sherman, was sworn, and, among other things, testified, "that Colonel Worthington had told him, shortly before leaving the camp at Shiloh, that he wanted to make a report of the Tennessee expedition, and throw the responsibility of our defeat where it belonged. He stated that it rested upon Generals Grant, C. F. Smith, and Sherman, and he was determined to show them up to the people of Ohio and the world."

This evidence shows that this treatise had its origin on the field of Shiloh, with no possible political bearing or purpose whatever. He did suspect from Halleck's words, few as they were, and his movements, slow as they were, that there was an influence beyond him and his coadjutors at work. If traced, as it is, to a cabal inside or outside the Cabinet, or war office, it is all the same to this relator, and had he traced that influence to his father's coffin, he would have torn it open all the same, to expose such hitherto unrecorded infamy, without regard to parties, circumstances, or men, dead or alive.

This dealing in human lives and limbs, and public safety, may have a petty parallel in the example of some seven by nine German duchy, whose prince sold his subjects to the king of England during our rebellion of the Revolution. This prince was not satisfied with anything but the death of his subjects wounded under the English contract for their blood and bones. If wounded, they came back upon his hands; if dead, they were paid for at so much a head. That was his "logic of events," and very conclusive pocket-logic it was. Perhaps it may have been one of the Lilliputs of Cassel, but whoever it was, it was no viler a bargain made by him with Britain than that between the "cabal" and these commanders. They were to carry out the "policy" and were to be carried through the war, as they were. It was the war that carried them along, not they who really carried on the war.

It was a clear case of Dundreary philosophy the tail became the biggest and accordingly wagged the dog, who was commanded therefore by his own tail and thus the last in merit are the first in place and power. It should be stated that, in April, 1862, the writer may have believed General C. F. Smith to blame for the affair of Shiloh, but he has long since discovered, and Halleck's dispatches show, that he was, in his illness and unfitness for duty, made the helpless instrument of a wicked purpose.

Occasion also is taken here to withdraw his charge against Sherman, of complicity with the enemy, made, not in defence of the charges against the prisoner, for he made none that would thwart his objects, one of which was to get out of such a command, but in defence of his diary extracts and their principles of war, and against Sherman's plain criminality on his own evidence.

He closed his unfinished defence as follows:

I did, in extreme cases, report to General Sherman, but all

social communion between us had ceased after the 19th of March, 1862, when I had reluctantly concluded that he was utterly unfit for his position, and he knowing that I knew it, I had nothing to expect but that he would disgrace myself and regiment, if he could, as has since occurred.

From what I heard from him within a week after my arrival at Paducah, I concluded that he could not safely be trusted with any 'separate and important command.' Every day has more and more and more confirmed this conviction; and if anything more was wanting, the manner in which this trial has been brought on———and the false and contradictory evidence given here by him, cumulate the conclusion that he is utterly unfit and incompetent for any responsible command.

Should he wish to change sides, he could bring ample arguments to show that his action has been unfavourable to the Union. ———I knew perfectly well that he knew of the rebel artillery in our front on the 5th of April; and how could he ignore the fact when he had heard those guns on Friday, which should have been hunted up on Saturday, as they were not. Saturday was by the rebels made a day of rest within cannon shot of our camp; and if there was ever an invitation to an enemy to make an attack, when, how, and where he chose, that invitation was given to the rebel army on the 5th and 6th of April, 1862, by Major General W. T. Sherman.

Sherman was engaged in a viler service than that of the enemy. In that, there might have been personal danger with doubtful advancement; in the other there was immediate advancement without other effort than that of mischief to the service, such as he afterwards wrought at Vicksburg, Jackson, Meridian, Chattanooga, Oostanaula, Kenesaw, Peach Tree creek, Durham station, and on many other occasions during the war.

He is absolved from all service in the rebel cause. It was much too honourable for such a man, as his evidence and acts have shown him to be.

Deerfield, Warren County, Ohio, January 11, 1872.
General T. Worthington, Morrow, Ohio.

Dear Sir: In answer to your inquiries, I have to say that I was assistant surgeon of the 20th Illinois Volunteer Infantry, Colonel C. C. Marsh, at the battle of Shiloh. That General Sherman was first seen by that regiment when his two centre brigades were driven past and through the left of General McClernand's camp, to the right and rear of his division, (the 1st,) about 9 a. m., April 6, 1862. That General W. T. Sherman, during the remainder of the day, kept in rear of his fragmentary troops, but did not seem at all active in rallying or encouraging them to any effort, simply holding his proper position, and nothing more, in the rear.

In the afternoon he and his staff were simply spectators of what was doing in McClernand's division, which, though much thinned out, kept well together till 4.30 p. m. I was at the landing on duty about 4 p. m., when Hurlbut's division was driven in. On returning to my proper position soon after, I found that immediately after Hurlbut's retreat the troops on our extreme right, fragments of Sherman's division, had been driven back towards Snake creek bridge, as stated in General Sherman's report. Besides the 17th and 20th Illinois, specified by General McClernand's report, as alone retaining their organization after 4 p. m., the 11th Illinois, though much reduced, kept well together. What troops were left of these three regiments at 5 p. m. would not have exceeded eight hundred men in line.

Much indignation was expressed after the battle at what was considered the negligence of Generals Sherman and Grant. No one imputed any effective action that day to General Sherman, and Colonels Marsh, Hare, Crocker, and many others, were considered, under General McClernand, as having been infinitely more efficient in keeping any troops in line till 5 p. m. than Sherman or Grant; the first a mere spectator, and the latter scarcely seen or even heard of anywhere on the field. As to General Grant, his utter incompetence was considered his excuse for allowing his army to be surprised and defeated. At Donelson his conduct, in keeping off the field, was the same. It was not disputed that had not Generals Buell and Nelson, with Colonel Ammen's force, arrived with assistance about 5 p. m., the Army of the Tennessee would have been dispersed or captured, as stated in General Grant's report. From a little after 5 p. m. till dark the firing on our extreme left was at least if not more severe than on any part of the field during the day.

Yours, respectfully,   G. W. Henderson,
                                        Ass't Surg. 20th Ill.V. I.

The above statement is verified by General McClernand, who, writing the same date from Springfield, Illinois, says:

Sherman's division, losing its organization in the morning, occupied no definite position from that time till near dark. In the meantime General Sherman was without any real command. Grant may have seen Sherman before or about noon without his division. I saw not General Grant, nor received word from him during the day.

CHAPTER 11

Grant on and off the Battlefield, and on his Boat at Noon

Grant was on every part of the field in person, constantly under fire, and making unwearied exertions to maintain his position until Nelson and Lewis Wallace should get up, but the national forces were losing ground every hour. (*Badeau's Life of Grant.*)

Grant was never discouraged, and rose to the height of a hero when the storm had burst. (Whitelaw Reid.)

Commanding Officer advance forces Buell's army.
    Near Pittsburgh, April 6, 1862, (near noon.)
If you will get upon the field, it will possibly save the day to us. The rebel forces are estimated at 100,000 men.
    U. S. Grant.

About 1 o'clock p. m., April 6, I reached Pittsburgh landing. I found Grant on his boat, with two or more of his staff, in the ladies' cabin. I proposed we should go ashore, and his horses were accordingly taken ashore.
    D.C. Buell.

Too much space has perhaps been devoted to the night before the battle, if too much attention can be paid to events which preceded the most inexplicable battle, and most far-reaching results of any one before on record. We now bring Grant on to the battlefield of Shiloh, where he achieves nothing but to discover that, in his conviction, it is lost, as will presently appear, and that he acted accordingly, and perhaps discreetly, and Hudibrastically.

As Lieutenant Moore says, Grant reached Pittsburgh about 10 a. m., perhaps a little before. He thence perhaps sent a verbal order to General Lew. Wallace, and the order to General Wood, recorded in Badeau's history. General Sherman says nothing about seeing him in his division report, till 3 p. m. In his letter of January, 1865, he says he saw him about 10 a. m. The time must have been half-past 10 or 11, as General Grant was seen by General Veatch on the Corinth road about that time. He must have seen Sherman while his first brigade was detached, as Sherman says, to join on McClernand's right.

Both doubtless gave up the brigade for lost, as nothing else seemed possible. Grant, however, saw that without speedy assistance the day was lost, beyond a peradventure. He returned to his headquarters near the landing about noon, or half an hour earlier, and there found fugitives from the extreme right of this detached brigade, which, with its commander, declared that the first brigade on the extreme right was broken and scattered, and the rebels would soon be at the landing. Whereupon he wrote as below, and despatched the note by a boat which passed Crump's landing, with a message for Wallace, about noon. General Buell, at any rate, got the note about that time, or a little later, on his way up to Pittsburgh landing. Here is the letter:

Commanding Officer advance forces Buell's army.

Near Pittsburgh, April 6, 1862, (noon.)

The attack on my forces has been very spirited since early this morning. The appearance of fresh troops on the field now would have a powerful effect, both by inspiring our men and disheartening the enemy. If you will get upon the field, leaving all your baggage on the east bank of the river, it will be a move to our advantage, and possibly save the day to us. The rebel forces are estimated at over 100,000 men. My headquarters will be in the log building on the top of the hill, where you will be furnished a staff officer to guide you to your place on the field.

      Respectfully,   U. S. Grant.

The first inference from the letter is plain, that the day is given up, without reinforcements, by which it can only possibly be saved. The second is, that if there are 100,000 men in his front, it will be but bringing men to "add to slaughter" to bring up Nelson's 6,000 or 7,000 troops. The third inference is, that the mention of these 100,000 hostile troops is intended, as it might be calculated, to keep reinforcements, of a force like Nelson's, back. The fourth is, that having left a staff officer to attend to the reinforcements, Grant has returned to the field, which by this note he had plainly given up for lost. If so, there was some chivalry in the deed. Badeau's history strengthens such an inference in the mind of a careless or admiring reader, as he says (page 80) "that Grant was on every part of the field in person, constantly under fire, and making unwearied exertions to maintain his position till Nelson and Lewis Wallace should get up. But the national forces were slowly losing ground each hour. Still, if only Nelson and Lewis Wallace would come up, the day might even yet be saved."

So that Grant was on the field, striving against impossibilities, if Wallace and Nelson did not come up, and very serious improbabilities if they did even get up in time.

Some one has written, that the struggle of a great-souled man against gigantic odds is a spectacle worthy the immortal gods.

Here, then, was an example: the ubiquitous Grant everywhere, with the might and terror of a Titan, piling Pelion upon Ossa, the fiery soul of Hector, and the sword of Achilles, and also the longbow of Ulysses, only to be drawn by Grant and Sherman, his long-bowman, with Badeau at hand with the thunderbolts of Jove—struggling, as it were, between Scylla and Charybdis, (or at any rate, between hawk and buzzard,) on that field embattled by an even mightier foe—it was "*tres grand—magnifique*" when at about 1 p. m., with himself and horses on his boat—the *Tigress*—with his cigar of course, and engaged in his usual and habitual recreation, Buell found him as follows:

Airdrie, Ky., Feb. 25, 1872.

It could not have been later than 1 o'clock p. m., when I arrived at Pittsburg landing, on the 6th of April. The steamer on which I was, landed almost against, but a little above, the one which Grant used. On inquiring for him, I was informed that he was on board his steamer. I went there, and found him in the ladies' cabin, with two, possibly three, officers of his staff, whose names I do not now remember, if even I ever knew. I did not particularly observe them. I understood that they had all Grant and his staff recently come in from the field. After getting what information I could from him, and arranging with him to send steamers to bring up Crittenden's division from Savannah, I proposed that we should go ashore. His horses were accordingly taken ashore.   D. C. Buell.

It is useless to waste time or strength, or ink or paper, drawing inferences, which draw themselves, like a cork without a screw, when you cut the string off.

It is very plain that it was no use, with less than 20,000 men, to struggle with 100,000 on such a field. He had found himself of no use there any how, which is more, by the loss of at least 5,000 men, than could be said for Sherman. Sherman was the ablest tactician at a drill, the oldest graduate, higher in military art in his class than Grant, and, what was more, had the most influence at "Washington; and Sherman had given at least two examples against hope. At 10 a. m., or earlier, Sherman had turned over his last brigade to his aids, who in turn had turned the brigade over to the enemy.

They in turn had nearly turned its right flank, and its commander had returned to the landing, and made such a report to Grant of the defeat, by the turning of the 46th Ohio and 6th Iowa on the right flank, that Grant, thinking it best to keep up appearances, wrote Nelson that, if he came to attack, he must expect to meet 100,000 men. Like a discreet commander and horse fancier, he thereupon, after turning over this weight of responsibility, turned his attention to his horses, and betook himself to his boat. What were his intentions remain, as the historical philosophers say, "enshrouded in the womb of time." His memories, however, most likely recurred to Fort Donelson, where he had found such comfort on Commodore Foote's gunboat, while the battle was raging above; and, perhaps, concluded that Floyd, when he left his command at Donelson, had, doubtless, done the best thing possible, under the circumstances. All inferences on this affair are deferred to a generous public, who may, or may not, suspend a conclusion.

Note. No charge of cowardice is here preferred, or so intended, against General Grant, who has. perhaps, the same courage of calculation held in common with practised soldiers or officers having a military education.

In absenting himself from the field, and keeping out of the battle; in neglecting to send for Buell's troops, whose arrival occurred at 10 a. m. of the 6th and noon of the 5th; in having all his boats at Pittsburgh, to prevent their coming up; in doing everything for a defeat, and nothing for victory, he was but carrying out his contract, or obeying orders, for which he has been paid in full long ago. Here is further proof that he expected the attack, while keeping Nelson back:

General Grant to General Buell.
Savannah, April 6, 1862.
General D. C. Buell: Heavy firing is heard up the (river,) indicating plainly that an attack has been made upon our most advanced positions. I have been looking for this, but did not believe the attack could be made be- fore Monday or Tuesday, 7th or 8th.
This necessitates my joining the forces up the river, instead of meeting you today, as I had contemplated.
I have directed General Nelson to move to the river with his division. He can march to opposite Pittsburgh.
Respectfully, your obedient servant,   U. S. Grant,
Maj. Gen. Commanding."

Appendix

For want of time and means, a large part of Chapter 9 is omitted, and also chapters headed "Sherman's Last Brigade," "Sherman on and off the Field," "Sherman's First Brigade," and "Sherman's Letter to the U. S. S. Magazine of January, 1865." These may appear in a future edition.

The following statements, part of the chapter as to Sherman on and off the Field, are given as all of that chapter for which there is present room or time:

Sherman's Report.

General Sherman having omitted to state in his report anything more as to what occurred when he was in front of Appler's regiment than that his orderly was killed, the omission is in some sort filled by Lieutenant Cutler's statement, in which all officers and men of the 53rd Ohio concurred. They were, however, deterred from signing with Cutler by fear of Sherman's resentment.

In a letter to Hon. Ben. Stanton, June 10, 1862, Sherman states that his orderly was killed 500 yards beyond Appler's regiment. Which statement is right?

Lieutenant Cutler's statement:

The undersigned hereby certifies, that in a speech made to the 53rd Ohio Volunteer Infantry, a few days after the battle of Shiloh, General Sherman said that Appler was a brave man; that he had told him (Sherman) that he did not order the regiment to retreat; that he would rather take Appler's word than that of the whole regiment, who were a pack of cowards; that it was true the regiment had been put in too exposed a position; that he had intended to alter it, but that, in consequence of their cowardice on the day of the battle, they should remain where they were. He said further, in connection with the battle, that Beauregard and A. S. Johnson were gentlemen and honourable men, (he knew them personally,) who would scorn to do a mean thing; that if the 53rd was attacked and retreated again, he would take as much pleasure in pouring shot and shell and canister into them as into the rebels.

I certify that the regiment was attacked at 7 a. m. on the 6th of April, (1862,) or a little before that time. General Sherman was just in front of the regiment when his orderly was killed, immediately on which he rode rapidly off toward the rear; that the regiment left the rear of its camp about twenty minutes afterwards, and General Sherman could not have seen and spoken to Colonel Appler in the camp as late as 8 a. m., (on the 6th,) or even an hour before that time. We further certify that it was General Sherman's wish that Appler should continue to command the regiment, and urged him to do so; but Colonel Appler declined on the ground that he did not think himself fitted for the command; and further, that from the left of Mungen's to the right of Appler's camp the distance was at least 300 yards, with low swampy ground between the camps, and to the left of the 53rd was an open field near a mile long, while there was thick brush not over 100 yards in front.

Also, that the artillery did not fire on the rebels as they crossed the valley, nor until half an hour after we were attacked.

Geo. E. Cutler,
First Lt. Co. G.,53rd O. V. I.

Memphis, Tens., Sept. 1, 1862.

The report of General Sherman states that McDowell conducted the attack on the enemy's left in good style.

The statement of his *aid-de-camp* (afterwards Lieutenant Colonel Upton, a gallant officer) shows how McDowell conducted the attack, and how near at the time General Sherman was to the extreme right, as he says he was, when he saw Grant at 10 a. m. of April 6, 1862:

I hereby certify that on the 6th of April, 1862, General Sherman was not seen by the 1st brigade of his division before the firing commenced, at about 7 a. m.; nor did I see him that day till at or about the time he ordered the brigade to fall back, about 2 p. m.

Also, that after the 46th regiment O. V. I. had fallen back after its first fire, about noon, I was, with Colonel McDowell, Captain Harland, Commissary Moreland, and Quartermaster Ingram, to the left of the brigade, on the edge of an open field, in which Taylor's battery, not then firing, was located. That there came suddenly a thick shower of balls, when I and Harland dismounted. Colonel McDowell and the quartermaster and commissary rode rapidly off towards the river, and I saw nothing more of Colonel McDowell for half an hour afterwards, also near Taylor's battery, Who said that his command was gone; that it was no use further exposing themselves, and they might as well go to the landing, towards which he immediately rode. Not far from the landing, near a battery, he was requested by Major ——, of the — regiment, to assist in rallying the broken troops; he remained doing so but a few moments. I knew nothing of hie having had a fall from his horse, but when he last rode away from the right of Taylor's battery he complained of having been hurt.

Edward N. Upton,
First Lt. Co. D., 46th Regt. O. V. I.

Camp No. 7, May 15, 1862.
Witness: Oliver P. Brown.

General Sherman, in his report, having stated that at 10 or 10-30 a. m. he drove back the rebel left and relieved the pressure on McClernand's front, by means of McDowell's 1st brigade, the statement of Major Smith tells how and how far this driving back was done, and how Sherman did it:

Camp Before Corinth, May 23, 1862

Major J. B. Smith, 40th Illinois, says that about noon on the 6th of April, 1862, the regiment came into an open field, near a Union battery, about 400 yards south of an old house in the north end of the field, where it was met by General W. T. Sherman. There, on consultation, or after conversation with Colonel Hicks, in which Sherman said there was a rebel battery before us he wished taken, he (Sherman) ordered the regiment forwards towards the same, General Sherman, as we started, being to the rear of the left flank. That after marching at quick time some 300 or 400 yards, we were ordered to halt and lie down on rising ground, in sight of the battery, not exceeding two hundred yards in front, which battery, however, was not seen when the regiment started.

We remained in this position some twenty or thirty minutes, when we fell back about 300 yards, when we were again rallied, and advanced about 100 yards, where we remained till ordered to retreat by an officer I did not know.

In the first advance we lost about 180 men, (including Colonel Hicks, badly wounded,) killed and wounded. After the first advance we lost about forty men.

After General Sherman's first order to advance I saw no more of him that day.   J. B. Smith,

Maj. 40th Ill.

T. Worthington, Col. 46A Ohio.

The most extraordinary statement in Sherman's report is, that at 10 a. m. Buckland and McDowell's brigades were conducted so as to join on McClernand's left flank. This is a fiction as regards Buckland's brigade, which, by his report, was utterly disorganized on the first retreat at 9 a. m. The single 1st brigade was then by him deserted, as he says, in the hottest of the fight, while he himself sought refuge under the rear of McClernand's right wing, the second desertion of his troops that morning by 9 a. m. This, as Badeau says, was "commanding McClernand's division, as well as his own."

Here, then, was W. T. Sherman, a West Point graduate of high-class grade, in command of a division of about 7,000 men, during a battle where there was more terror, confusion, and bloodshed combined, than any other fought within this century, or perhaps any other, who abandons his only available troops to his subordinates at a time when a skillful commander was most wanted; when, as he reports, regiments, brigades, and divisions were successively swept back, and the most trifling accident might drive back McClernand in slaughter and confusion, he thus exposes this remnant of his troops, this forlorn hope of the army, as it turned out to be, to seemingly inevitable destruction.

Who would believe it, if not in his report; yet in this one respect that report is true, except that these troops were not permitted by the enemy to join McClernand's right, nor did he expect it. From 9 a. m. till 2 p. m. this deserted force, with the loss of near half its number, or 700 men, prevented the turning of the Union right flank, and prevented its being driven back till 2 p. m. that day, without aid or encouragement from Sherman or its brigadier.

Joke on Sherman

An odd statement, and, still more oddly, a true one, of Sherman's report, that it would have been madness to have exposed horses to the musketry fire of the two days' battle to which he so freely exposed his men more especially those of the first brigade, turned over, he says, in the hottest of the fight to his aides in derogation of himself: this characteristic benevolence, so like Grant, for his horses, taken together with the evidence of Colonel Stuart, that his artillery would have been captured on the 6th had it not been taken back on the 5th April, started a joke among the wags in camp, that Sherman had withdrawn Ins artillery lest it should be captured, and his cavalry lest the horses should be hurt. Though so much more careful of the horses while living, all were treated with the same neglect when dead buried, or covered up, where they fell. Very inconsistent and contradictory conduct, but just like the "Great Commander" W. T. Sherman.

GRANT'S CONTRADICTIONS

The following letter from General Grant is in direct contradiction of his report that Buell's troops saved the landing, transports, &c., from capture. April 6, 1862, and is part of one of the chapters excluded for want of room, &c.

Washington, D. C., April 7, 1872

General W. W. Belknap:

Give my congratulations to the gallant Society of the Army of the Tennessee, and regrets that public duty prevented my being with them on the anniversary of one of the hardest-fought battles of the rebellion. The battle of Shiloh, though much criticized at the time, will ever be remembered by those engaged in it as a "brilliant success," won with raw troops over a superior force, and under circumstances the most unfavourable to the Union troops.

U. S. Grant.

Grant's force was not less than 53,000, purposely scattered ten or eleven miles along the river, by two or three miles back. The Confederates had less than 41,000 men. The "unfavourable circumstances" had been purposely arranged by himself. The "brilliant success" was a disgraceful defeat, which, but for Buell, Nelson, and Ammen, would have been entire capture or rout of the Union army, devoted by him to ruin.

GRANT'S NOTICE OF "SHILOH" AND
WHAT COMES OF IT.

Before the last pages of this incomplete work went to press, and on the morning that Grant's notice of Shiloh appeared in the Washington Republican, the writer found that a resolution of the House as to missing rebellion records applied only to that of Buell's court of inquiry. He thereupon returned thanks for the notice to the proper editor of the Republican (Grant) in writing; and in order that the President might try conclusions as to the "missing records," if he chose, before the highest national tribunal, he presented to Congress the memorial as follows:

Washington, D. C., May 24, 1872.

To the Congress of the United States:

This relator respectfully presents, for reference only, a treatise on the Tennessee or Shiloh campaign of 1862, to prove that the campaign was mainly fruitless after February, 1862, by reason of the policy for protracting the war previously adopted; and also to prove that for the purpose of such protraction, the defeat of the Union army at Shiloh, April 6, 1862, was the result of that policy, carried out under direction of the late General Halleck by General Grant.

The first overt act for continuing the war in Tennessee, against all military principles, one year or more, was perfected by the order of March 12, 1862, placing General Buell under the immediate command of General Halleck, who permitted the junction of A. S. Johnson's army from Decatur with the rebel army at Corinth, resulting in the disaster to the Union army at Shiloh April 6, 1862. Evidence of the first overt act to secure that defeat is found in the dispatches of General Halleck of March 3rd and 4th, herein submitted. These dispatches are fictitious and deceptive on their face, and intended to place the responsibility for the position of the battlefield of Shiloh on C. F. Smith.

This protractive policy, and its terrible consequences, required the suppression or destruction of all special army records, and the entire abrogation of all established principles and practice of military law, of which this relator has ample evidence, as to the Shiloh campaign of 1862. No such records can be had at the War Department, for they are not there.

The dispatches of General Halleck, March 3 and 4, 1862, to the War Department and to General Grant, are authenticated in Badeau's military life of Grant. General Halleck's dispatch of March 4th to General Buell was obtained from General Buell himself.

For the purpose of obtaining a correct history of this campaign, never yet published, this relator respectfully suggests and requests that a competent commission be at once appointed to rescue from destruction such army records as remain, and replace as far as possible those abstracted from the War Department at Washington, D. C.

    Respectfully,   T. Worthington,
Late Colonel 46th Regiment Ohio Volunteer Infantry.

The writer earnestly requests all honourable soldiers and good citizens to sign and forward this and the above memorial to the next Congress, and to their State Legislatures:

                       Washington, May 30, 1872

To the Congress of the United States.

The undersigned respectfully submits (for aiding reference to official evidence only) a treatise on the Tennessee campaign of 1862, the special records of which have hitherto been suppressed or removed from the War Department. He requests that, by an appropriate commission, there may be an examination into the truth of the matter stated in said treatise, to determine:—

1st. Whether the war of the rebellion in Tennessee in 1862 was not purposely continued one year, or more, for purposes outside of the prosecution of the war; and whether, in the year 1862, the usual rules of war in this campaign, and all established military law, were not utterly disregarded.

2nd. Whether the disaster to the Union army at Shiloh, April 6, 1862, was not the result of design on the part of one or more officers of the United States army, including the officer then in command of the Army of the Tennessee.

3rd. Whether the evidence given by General W. T. Sherman, and his conduct during the battle as stated in his division report, is such as renders such an officer a safe depositary of his present command of the national army.

4th. Whether there should not be such additions made to the Army Regulations and the Articles of War as will guard against the acts and neglects stated in the treatise herewith submitted.

5th. Whether the Judge Advocate General properly performed his duty in taking no notice of such evidence on the part of a commander and prosecutor as that set forth in the treatise.

6th. Whether, from any lapse of time, an examination into the offences charged should be remitted, and whether there is or not any redress for the proven wrong inflicted, without offence against the Army Regulations or Articles of War.

7th. Whether the officers named as offenders in the treatise hold their present positions by meritorious conduct, or by collusion with those in power at Washington intrusted with the conduct of the war in 1862.

T. Worthington,
Late Col. 46th Regt. O. V. I.

WARNING TO THE PEOPLE AGAINST THEIR LEADERS IN ANY FUTURE WAR, AND AGAINST FAITH IN MEN OF MERELY MILITARY REPUTATION.

Since the issue of the first chapter of "Shiloh," the writer has observed that the crimes proven therein, without ground of denial, are considered of so terrible and atrocious a character, that most intellects shrink in horror from their contemplation.

If there was any room for doubt or extenuation, any excuse or explanation, the treatise on Shiloh would be largely quoted and have a wide circulation at once. But the military crime of giving fictitious and deceptive information in an invasive war, and of continuing the same at the expense of so many hundreds of millions of money and rivers of blood the deliberate location of an army on a field chosen for its slaughter— the studied preparation of at least one army, by its commander, for destruction and disgrace—the deliberate desertion of 'their troops in obedience to a cruel policy, by one or more commanders, at the moment of greatest danger, and the brutal consignment of their victims to scattered, shallow, and nameless graves, where they fell, constitute crimes which, if recognized, separate their perpetrators from all social intercourse and all human sympathy with honourable men.

Such crimes, of the most atrocious and basest description, were denominated under the general term of *"perduellium"* by the Roman law. The crimes of these men are too monstrous for record in any modern criminal calendar. For such horrors nothing is left but silence as to their perpetrators, and thus through their infinite atrocity they escape unpunished. And not only that, but, to avoid the unfolding of such terrible records, such guiltiest of men are allowed to hold the highest civil and military positions in the Republic, and with the multitude to live on with the reputation of "characters" whom the people have delighted to honour.

WARNING!

"If such there be, the moral of this work."

First. The most intelligent people on earth may, for more than ten years together, be deluded by their trusted political leaders, as to the means and manner of conducting a civil war.

Second. Men with no merit as soldiers, and with less than none as generals, may be imposed upon this nation and the world as the greatest commanders of the age.

Therefore it is the conviction of this writer, that we know and care less about military laws and affairs, and are the merest politicians and money-grabbers of the world.

A state of affairs producing such generals and rulers as Halleck, Grant, and Sherman, distinguished for nothing, but worse than good-for-nothingness.

A state of affairs dangerous in the extreme, but even productive of future benefit, if it can teach us how worthless is military reputation, and bow exceedingly to be avoided in the choice of our rulers.

GRATEFUL CONCLUSION

Grant having impudently set forth in his "organ," of May 24th, inst., that this relator of hidden history is "on agency set in operation," and "a man put forward" to disclose the infamy of "eminence," he therefore avers what may easily be proven, that he has had nothing but discouragement and disapprobation from nearly all, and direct commendation from but two subscribers to his work—perhaps but one.

He is under the greatest obligations to two school-mates of fifty years ago, both now United States Senators, and to his printer especially, for getting on so far with an imperative professional and public duty, which no one else on earth could have performed.

His depth of obligation to all who have made advances at such risk cannot be expressed in words, but may be conjectured, when he avers that for months together, and most of the time since 1862, he has subsisted on a peck of corn meal a week for himself and dog, with a pound of lard for his griddle, say 25 cents, or less, "and water from the spring," without even the hermit's "scrip with herbs and fruits supplied." This he has done, that he might urge his claims each winter for army supplies furnished his own regiment and other troops in 1861, and obtain, if possible, an investigation of the case, now submitted to the people as the court of last resort in all cases whatever.

LEONAUR

ALSO FROM LEONAUR

AVAILABLE IN SOFTCOVER OR HARDCOVER WITH DUST JACKET

WELLINGTON AND THE PYRENEES CAMPAIGN VOLUME I: FROM VITORIA TO THE BIDASSOA *by F. C. Beatson*—The final phase of the campaign in the Iberian Peninsula.

WELLINGTON AND THE INVASION OF FRANCE VOLUME II: THE BIDASSOA TO THE BATTLE OF THE NIVELLE *by F. C. Beatson*—The second of Beatson's series on the fall of Revolutionary France published by Leonaur, the reader is once again taken into the centre of Wellington's strategic and tactical genius.

WELLINGTON AND THE FALL OF FRANCE VOLUME III: THE GAVES AND THE BATTLE OF ORTHEZ by *F. C. Beatson*—This final chapter of F. C. Beatson's brilliant trilogy shows the 'captain of the age' at his most inspired and makes all three books essential additions to any Peninsular War library.

NAVAL BATTLES OF THE NAPOLEONIC WARS *by W. H. Fitchett*—Cape St.Vincent, the Nile, Cadiz, Copenhagen, Trafalgar & Others

SERGEANT GUILLEMARD: THE MAN WHO SHOT NELSON? *by Robert Guillemard*—A Soldier of the Infantry of the French Army of Napoleon on Campaign Throughout Europe

WITH THE GUARDS ACROSS THE PYRENEES by *Robert Batty*—The Experiences of a British Officer of Wellington's Army During the Battles for the Fall of Napoleonic France, 1813.

A STAFF OFFICER IN THE PENINSULA *by E. W. Buckham*—An Officer of the British Staff Corps Cavalry During the Peninsula Campaign of the Napoleonic Wars

THE LEIPZIG CAMPAIGN: 1813—NAPOLEON AND THE "BATTLE OF THE NATIONS" *by F. N. Maude*—Colonel Maude's analysis of Napoleon's campaign of 1813.

BUGEAUD: A PACK WITH A BATON by *Thomas Robert Bugeaud*—The Early Campaigns of a Soldier of Napoleon's Army Who Would Become a Marshal of France.

TWO LEONAUR ORIGINALS

SERGEANT NICOL by *Daniel Nicol*—The Experiences of a Gordon Highlander During the Napoleonic Wars in Egypt, the Peninsula and France.

WATERLOO RECOLLECTIONS by *Frederick Llewellyn*—Rare First Hand Accounts, Letters, Reports and Retellings from the Campaign of 1815.

www.ingramcontent.com/pod-product-compliance
Lightning Source LLC
Chambersburg PA
CBHW021057090426
42738CB00006B/391